*To Alan
Best
Wishes*

Alan Perna

Concept & design by Skip Johnston

skipjohnstondesign@gmail.com

Edited by Anna Leigh Clem

aapertura@gmail.com

All content is the property of the author/photographer
and is not to be reprinted without the owners permission.

To Alan Best Wishes

Obsessed with celebrities, a Brooklyn teen comes of age collecting autographs in Broadway's Shubert Alley.

Alan Perna

Sandra Dee autographing Alan's book outside Sardi's

CONTENTS

9 **Brooklyn**
"In the 1950s Brooklyn was a very provincial town."

14 **My Parents**
"When I thought I had outgrown them, my mother and father rescued my photographs and autographs from the trash can."

21 **The Collectors**
"My connection to show business and its celebrities was through my collecting."

36 **Friendships**
"My social life was shared with a close group of collectors."

40 **Photographs**
Collection of fifty taken in 1958.

67 **Autographs**
Collection of four hundred acquired between 1955 and 1958.

133 **Acknowledgments**

We waited for Marilyn outside her East 57th Street apartment the night of the opening of *Some Like It Hot*

8

BROOKLYN

With my mother and little brother Bob

In 1955 I was 13. I had already sung in choirs and danced in amateur recitals.

> I guess I assumed my future was in show business. So while everyone else my age was going through puberty, I stumbled upon a group of people who were hanging out in the theatre section and following celebrities. For me it was a combination of coming out and coming of age. It only lasted 3 years, until I was 16, but it was one of the happiest periods of my life.

Brooklyn

Dressed for a Brooklyn Academy of Music recital, where I sang "The Star Spangled Banner"

I grew up in Brooklyn in the 1940s and 50s. At that time, Brooklyn was a very provincial town. If you weren't into sports, you hung out on street corners or in candy stores around the jukebox. I watched American Bandstand while I did my homework and practiced dance steps holding on to the doorjamb.

By the age of two my mother had enrolled me in tumbling class. I attended The Immaculate Heart of Mary, a Catholic grammar school taught by the Sisters of St. Joseph. While studying tap, ballet and acrobatics with Miss Lee at the Windsor Terrace School of Dance, I also sang in the church choir. The students, boys and girls, ranged in age from very young to teenagers. At dance school recitals there were always more girls than boys, so the girls were given the dressing rooms, while the boys had to change beneath the stairwell. This was very embarrassing! We were taught routines set to popular music which, at the end of each school year, we performed at recital halls; once it was held at the Brooklyn Academy of Music.

I opened the show singing "The Star Spangled Banner" in a white dinner jacket. With my voice changing at thirteen—I cracked! At the end of each recital, Miss Lee would perform her solo tap dance in her lucky chartreuse dress. She was very good and very pretty. Her long, dark hair would be pulled up in a knot, her lips and shoes were bright red and she would smile, then spin and "spot" very fast. I thought she was great.

WINDSOR TERRACE

SCHOOL OF DANCING

presents

Broadway Memories

MASONIC TEMPLE

Lafayette and Clermont Aves.

Saturday, June 20, 1953

8:30 P.M.

— STUDIO —

26 EAST 3rd STREET

Brooklyn 18, N. Y.

SOuth 8-9753

A publicity shot for one of our numbers - that's me on the far left

Each June, between tests and summer vacation, we held our end of school recitals. Miss Kay and Mr. Bowness arrived in the spring to help us prepare. She arranged the choreography, he played the piano. Costumes were made followed by fittings and rehearsals. I can still remember the smell and feel of wet pancake make up.

My grade school knew that I was learning routines in dancing school, so each year they would ask to see what I had learned and ask me to do a solo. They would work it into the show, it made things easier for them. After playing Dopey in Snow White I was called Dopey for years after.

Moving on to St. Michaels, an all boys Catholic prep school, I left behind art classes, but the Xaverian Brothers did offer music and I continued dance outside of school; ballroom this time.

MY PARENTS

My father's varied interests, among them photography and music, taught me and
my brother an appreciation for the arts.

    Yet while my father never approved of my dance studies—I believe he was concerned about the "effect" it might have on me socially—in later years he was disappointed I hadn't continued with my singing because, as he said to me, I had a "very good" voice.

    For a quiet man, that was high praise.

My father outside our apartment on East 4th St., Brooklyn

My mother's early enthusiasm for the arts and entertainment were expressed through me: as I grew older, many of the experiences we shared and the dreams we had, were on Broadway.

Portrait of my mother, probably taken by my father when they were courting

When I was young, my mother and I would make frequent trips into Manhattan to shop or see a show. On one excursion, as we passed the 21 Club, my mother said to me, *"There's Senator Kennedy. Get his autograph."*

She was very excited. I didn't know who he was, but he gave me his autograph when I asked. It was my first, now yellowed and stained. I have it framed.

It reads, *"To Alan, John Kennedy."*

My Parents

We had another memorable day that began on West 52nd, watching *Sweet Smell of Success* being filmed; Burt Lancaster and Tony Curtis were on the set. It was the first time I had seen one being made. It was a night scene and I remember between takes the sanitation trucks kept hosing down the street to make it look like it had rained.

On the way home we passed the Palace Theater where Judy Garland was appearing; we were both fans. By chance we went to the side street and found a black metal door. Through it we could hear Judy singing and talking to the audience. We stood listening for a long time.

Many years later, my mother would wait again for Judy, on line outside the Frank Campbell Funeral Home.

Once I was standing on the steps of the Plaza Hotel when Judy Garland ran past me, down the stairs into a waiting limo. She was very petite and it was during her 'fat' period—she was wearing a black cape, a large black picture hat and had very pointed eyebrows. I ran up to the car and tapped on the window. She turned; I said "I love you." She smiled and mouthed "Thank you."

My mother in my room on Vanderbilt St. I was 17 - it was the first time I had my own room, the biggest in the apartment

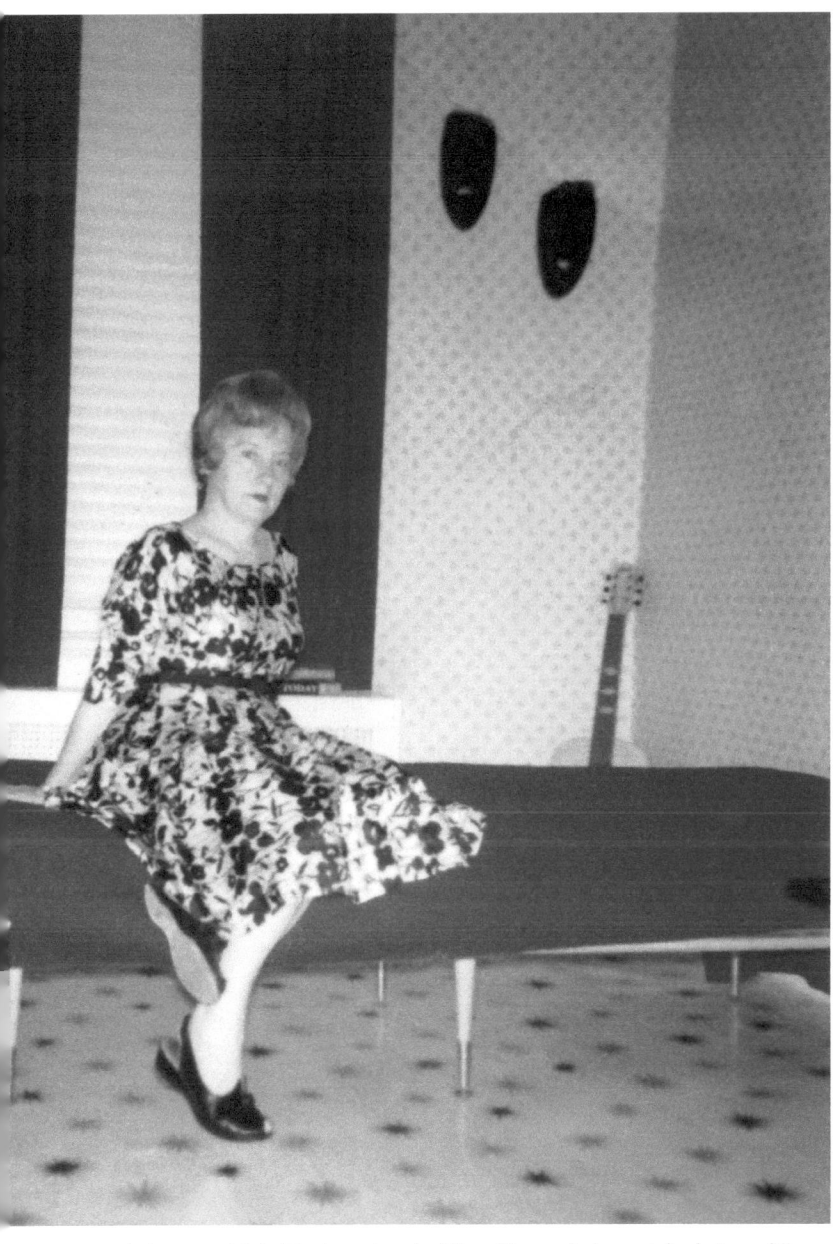

I decorated it in black, red and white with a pole lamp, tub chair and "comedy and tragedy" masks

At twenty-two I decided I had outgrown my autograph collection and celebrity photographs and threw them out. Fortunately my mother salvaged the autographs and my father saved the photos. Thanks to both of them I still have a collection.

20

THE COLLECTORS

My connection to show business and its celebrities was through my collecting.

From left: Arthur Miller, Marilyn Monroe, Cyril Ritchards, George MacDonald and me

The Collectors

Every morning my mother listened to Arthur Godfrey on the radio. She went with friends to see his show several times, coming home with a bag of free samples and stories of the cast members. I began to write away for tickets. When I had free time I would go to the NBC studios in the RCA building at Rockefeller Center, complimentary tickets for the day's shows were available. After the shows I waited at the stage door to have my programs signed.

At thirteen I was too young to travel alone to evening shows like *Masquerade Party*, so my mother would accompany me into the city. On that particular evening, cued up at the stage door, for the first time I became aware of the collectors. Unlike excited fans or tourists, they were more serious, part of an inside network.

I met George MacDonald, a kid about my age, also in high school.
We agreed to meet the next day and hang out. He explained his collecting routine, including the best places to find celebrities. Together we discovered the group; there were teenagers like us, in school, collecting every free moment, and an older group working during the day and showing up for openings and special events in the evenings. Others who didn't collect hung around for the gossip. And along with them, some disturbing and embarrassing characters.

Tommy Murray (left), Unknown, Marsha Swinicki, Roger Rothberg with glasses, John Tase, Gwen and me

it can be *lonely* (continued)

a Hollywood column that I was going to Hollywood to make a test for Universal. And now we come back to that matter of me on the big soundstage. . . . So there I was at last, more alone, I guess, than I have ever felt in my whole life. There were a few men working overhead, pounding things and fixing lights—I don't really know what they were doing. They could have been Men from Mars for all of me. They didn't even notice me.

I walked around, trying to tell myself that I wasn't the only girl in the world who ever *(Continued on page 91)*

*I have spurts of confidence, like when I got all dressed up and went
see myself in "The Wonderful Years," hoping somebody would recogni
me in the lobby, maybe. Nobody did. But after the picture had been pla
ing around a while, people started noticing me. It was such a funny feelin*

Even when people are nice enough to ask for an autograph or stare in a restaurant, you keep wondering if they're really

Meeting up with other collectors was fairly casual and often unpredictable, but you were more than likely to run into each other in "The Alley." A little oasis in the theater district: Shubert Alley is a pedestrian walkway shortcut flanked by theaters lined with huge posters of current Broadway shows. It connects W.44th St. to W.45th St., halfway between Broadway and 8th Avenue. At the Shubert Theater, **Judy Holliday** was doing *Bells Are Ringing* with **Sydney Chaplin**. Next door at the Broadhurst, **Rosalind Russell** was starring in *Auntie Mame*. (Each evening when she left the theater her chaffeur would blink the limo's headlights at the collectors in front of Sardi's: at least that's what we believed.) **Ethel Merman** and **Fernando Lamas** were at The Majestic in *Happy Hunting* across the street from the St. James Theater's *L'il Abner* with **Edie Adams, Peter Palmer, Charlotte Rae, Stubby Kaye** and **Julie Newmar** (Many matinee days I watched **"Stupefyin Jones" Newmar** walk the length of W.44th St. with the eyes of the truckers from the N.Y. Times following her every step. Tall with a flowing mane of red hair, she wore a short camel-colored coat tied at the waist that accentuated her very long legs.) Classic Broadway was just around a corner; **Lena Horne** in *Jamaica*, *Inherit the Wind* with **Paul Muni** and **Edward G. Robinson** starring in *The Middle of the Night*, **Charles Laughton** and **Glynis Johns** in *Major Barbara*, *Moon for the Misbegotten* with **Franchot Tone**, **Teresa Wright** in *Dark at the Top of the Stairs*, **Rex Harrison** and **Julie Andrews'** incomparable *My Fair Lady*, **Florence Eldridge** and **Frederick March** in *A Long Day's Journey*, and **Carol Lawrence, Larry Kert** and **Chita Rivera** in *West Side Story*. I often find myself reflecting on the fact that while I was collecting there were four brilliant and creative men working together in the Broadway theatre: Leonard Bernstein, Stephen Sondheim, Arthur Laurents and Jerome Robbins. I wasn't aware of it at the time but teams like this don't come along that often.

Part of the time there was spent covering the shows, standing in front of theaters, scanning faces, watching for limos. Of course you could only cover one show at a time, other collectors were covering other shows and you would meet while the shows were in progress and could then cover a different show at intermission or wander in, find a seat and see the rest of the show. I saw a lot of second acts that way. I'd plan going from one show to another, waiting to see the stars and have a program signed.

Little did I know how much time, over the next three years, I would spend waiting.

Here I am in the May 1956 issue of Photoplay Magazine getting Sandra Dee's autograph in front of Sardi's, where I spent many hours waiting

The Collectors

26

At 16, with Cooky in Shubert Alley

Sardi's
I spent many cold and hungry hours outside Sardi's restaurant waiting to see who might go in or out. It's still a popular meeting place for a meal or drinks before or after a performance. Many actors patronize the place because the original owner, Vincent Sardi, helped struggling actors before they made it. There was a steady stream of familiar faces who were always working in the area — David Merrick, Arthur Laurents, Jerome Robbins and Adolph Green. There were the casts and crews of the currently playing shows and celebrities in town to see those shows. Ray Heatherton hosted a radio program from Sardi's every weekday at noon called *Luncheon at Sardi's*, during which he would interview people in town to plug a show, a film or a book. More than once I would be listening to the show at home and rush to the city to see the guest, only to find the show had been taped on another day! For all the hours I spent outside that restaurant, it would be a decade or more before I saw the inside.

The Actors Studio
Marlon Brando and Geraldine Page studied Method acting with Lee Strasberg. Every Tuesday morning at ten Marilyn Monroe arrived in a cab, fur coat draped over a turtleneck sweater, dark glasses and no make-up. I remember stopping a young Paul Newman with bleached blond curly hair, straddling a motorcycle outside the theater during the run of *Sweet Bird of Youth*. They said he looked too much like Brando to amount to anything.

Hotels
Collectors were usually up on who was in town to promote their latest effort and where they were staying; stars tended to stay at the same hotels. There was a newspaper called Show Business, which had a column listing celebrities in town and their hotels. Sometimes the info was right and sometimes not. Often by the time the paper came out, the celebrities had left town. Once you got used to spending boring hours alone, tired and hungry in all weather, hotels could be a refuge. More often than not the doormen would ask us to leave. I did have a friend in the doorman at the St. Regis. He was a big Irishman in a dark green uniform; a glass cubicle protected him from the rain and the cold. When I visited he would wave me right in, eager to see what autographs I had gotten that night. Arranging them just so, he would copy each of them exactly with a very strong calligraphic hand. I chose to keep only those autographs that were signed in front of me. At one point I had the Duke and Duchess of Windsor on Waldorf Astoria stationery as they were living there at the time, but a doorman had gotten it for me and I couldn't be sure it was real. Still, I wish now I had kept it. I continued being ushered out of the Plaza Hotel by the house detective more times than I care to remember. But if you had the nerve, you could call a celebrity directly on the house phone and ask when they might be coming down. Sometimes you would be invited up. Both Cesar Romero and Will "Sugarfoot" Hutchins extended *invitations*.

The 50s were a different time and I was very young.

When a celebrity finally arrived, things began to happen very quickly; pushing and shoving to give them your card and pen. While shooting their picture, another collector would take the opportunity to "crash" your shot.

This was annoying at the time, but now it's *almost* charming.

Noel Coward and Marlene Dietrich with Al Matthews

Joan Collins with Marsha Swinicki   John Tase "crashing" Cyd Charisse   May Britt with Al Matthews and Jimmy Leggi

I was waiting outside a rehearsal studio one day when someone I recognized passed in a taxi. I ran after the cab for three blocks until it stopped at a light. My heart was pounding, my mouth was dry. Opening the door and getting inside was really out of character for me, but I knew it was Tab Hunter I had been chasing, and was he ever surprised.

                                                                                 I asked for his autograph.

"I'll meet you back at the hotel," he said.

    I got out shaking, and as the cab drove off, it occurred to me I had no idea where he was staying; but was impressed by how calmly he had gotten rid of me.

        I've often wondered if he remembers that time.

Tab Hunter outside a rehearsal studio on 6th Ave.

Bob and Natalie on their honeymoon in New York

When Bob Wagner and Natalie Wood came to New York to have their first honeymoon, me and my friend Marsha Swinicki got to know them pretty well. We ran into them so often we began to follow them around the city, watching people's reactions as they recognized them. They made such a great looking couple.

>They seemed glamorous and so much older.
>We were just scruffy high school kids, although I think Natalie was only nineteen.

Bob and Natalie   Natalie and me

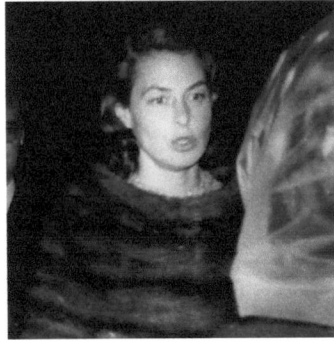

From the celebrities' vantage point we probably looked like a bothersome, if not frightening, band of people. Like animals stalking their prey, we would chase and surround them, thrusting pens, books and papers, asking questions and shooting pictures.

After the long wait — the sudden appearance, the confusion and then the calm, both predator and prey were satisfied.

Ingrid's return to the United States after a long interlude

George getting Ingrid's autograph

Ingrid with some of the collectors; John Reilly (third from left), Warren Thomas, Frank Yanosik, Red Currie (far right)

FRIENDSHIPS

Collecting was also my social life.

At one of the collectors' parties with unknown "soldier"

The collectors didn't just collect either — we went on outings together —like night swimming at Astoria Pool and day-long boat rides to Rye Beach. On one trip we took over the top rear deck, put our chairs in a large circle and sang show tunes. **Vinny Lo Preto** was the master of ceremonies. He and his sister **Ronnie** entertained us with every song from every musical with improvised choreography. I remember an unusually bumpy version of Marilyn Monroe's "Heat Wave".

My first collecting friend, **George MacDonald** was very preppy; sport coat, khakis and white bucks. He claimed to speak Latin fluently. His standard line to convince someone reluctant to sign was "I've seen every movie you ever made." He tried it once on Katharine Hepburn but she was known to be diffcult. **Tommy Murray** was in high school like George and I, a Brooklyn boy with sandy brown hair in his eyes, cigarette in his mouth, shirttail hanging out of his pants; not the usual type to be spending his time chasing stars. Unfortunately he was killed in a car crash somewhere in Rhode Island before he was twenty. We all met in the Alley, unable to believe it was Tommy and not knowing what else to do. **Cooky Morales** was a Cuban American girl from Jersey City, attractive, with long dark hair and a slapstick sense of humor. She was usually accompanied by her mother; we were all still under sixteen. She had the unfortunate habit of falling for gay guys, of which we had an ample supply. I eventually took her to my high school prom. **Roger Rothberg** was tall and rather gawky, with black horn rimmed glasses and a self deprecating sense of humor. He once asked Paul Newman for his autograph while standing next to him at a urinal. **Marsha Swinicki** wore braces. She and I got to know Natalie Wood and Bob Wagner when they were in New York on their honeymoon. **Rhoda Kuflick,** unlike the rest of us, carried an autograph book; *no one* carried autograph books except for her. She carried everything she owned in two large satchels. The problem was Rhoda collected *everything*. She couldn't use quarters, because she collected quarters. She couldn't use dimes, because she collected dimes. I pictured Rhoda's life coming to a complete standstill one day. When I met **another collector,** I was thirteen and he was eighteen. He joined the army and we corresponded for years. I saw him whenever he was home on leave. On my eighteenth birthday he took me to my first gay bar. The place was somewhere in Queens behind a storefront and down a dark flight of stairs. It was like being in a speak-easy. I had never seen men dancing together before. This was a time when the police regularly carted the patrons off in vans. It was very exciting! **Jack Custer** was one of the older collectors. He was very enthusiastic and knowledgeable about older, obscure, and foreign stars in particular. Sometimes he would ask one of us to shoot a "crotch shot" (top of the head to the knees) of a young, up and coming actor or chorus boy. There were fringe characters too, like **Celia Gordon** and her mother. I can see Celia now in leopard and black velvet. Leopard hat, black velvet coat with leopard trim, shoes and bag to match, a kind of thrift shop look. Her mother was always with her, a gray haired, crone-like woman from another century, and always screaming at Celia. **Barbara** was well spoken, obviously educated but distracted, with a lazy eye and a runny nose. Architecturally she was shaped like a pear and slanted backward. She walked with a purposeful almost swaggering stride, one arm clutching a newspaper, the other swinging her purse. And that purse could be a weapon if she thought you were making fun of her. **Dave** — called "Dirty Dave" — was loud, aggressive and hard to lose. He would approach people saying, "I know you. Aren't you somebody?" Once he tried to remove Grace Kelly's sunglasses while her hands were full so that we could take her picture. She was not pleased. Then there was **Rose, Helen, Tony, Joe, Lou, Walter, Red, Jimmy,** and many more.

Cooky's birthday party
Top left: Red, Walter, unknown, Vinnie and Rosemary   Bottom left: me, Bobby, Cooky, Ronnie and Sal

THE PHOTOGRAPHS

With my purchase of a Kodak Brownie Starflash, I began shooting photographs in '58, my last year of collecting.

Marlene Dietrich in Shubert Alley

Marilyn Monroe with Arthur Miller opening night for *Some Like It Hot*

Mary Martin, Gloria Swanson and Claudette Colbert in a Rolls Royce after theater at the Lunt Fontaine

Myrna Loy

Gwen Verdon and Bob Fosse

The Photographs

46

Susan Strasberg

Dorothy and Lillian Gish

Eartha Kitt

Luise Rainer

Connie Stevens

The Photographs

50

Kim Novak double exposure with Luise Rainer

Kim Novak

The Photographs

52

Jeanne Crain and Jane Powell

Peggy Wood

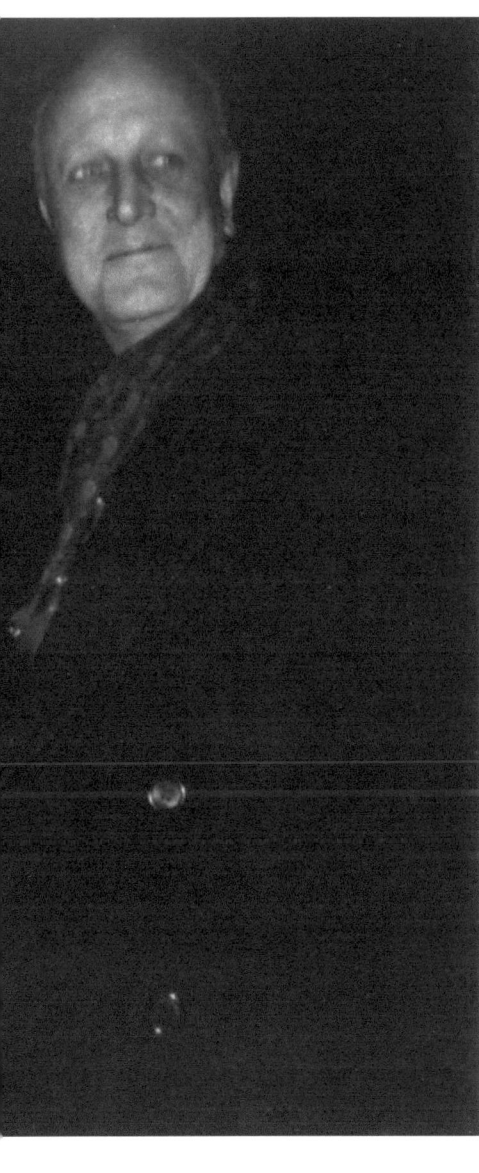

Judson Laire

Jeannie Carson and Margaret O'Brien

The Photographs

54

Brandon DeWilde

John Russell, (C. Unknown), James Garner

Paulette Goddard

Rosemary Clooney

The Photographs

58

June Allyson and Dick Powell

Ida Lupino and Howard Duff

The Photographs

Helen Hayes and son James MacArthur

Zsa Zsa Gabor

Fay Spain

Jane Wyman

Celeste Holm

The Photographs

Grace Kelly

Unknown

THE AUTOGRAPHS

From 1955 through '58 I collected well over 400 autographs, from Edie Adams to Dick York.

Me, a Mid-Century teen, in front of my east 4th Street home in Brooklyn

For me collecting was an obsession. Once you've committed yourself to waiting for someone, you can't bring yourself to leave. *"I know they're inside, they have to come out. They couldn't have gotten past me, I would have seen them."* Or they're about to arrive in the next cab or limo. You've already invested so much time, missed lunch and dinner, and called home to beg for *more* time.

Your eyes keep searching. Then suddenly, there they are, someone you've never set eyes on in person yet somehow feel you know.

You're looking at them, they're looking at you.
Smiling, you ask for an autograph: They ask your name. You take their picture.
Everything happens very quickly and then they're gone.
Finally, you get to go home happy.

Alfred Hitchcock's autograph

LTCW: Tab Hunter, Brandon de Wilde, Cliff Robertson, Forrest Tucker, Hugh O'Brian, Ethel Waters, Ernie Kovacs, Lena Horne, C. David Burns

LTCW: Anthony Quale, Edie Adams, Jaye P. Morgan, Tennessee Ernie Ford, John Cassavetes, Katherine Cornell, William Shattner

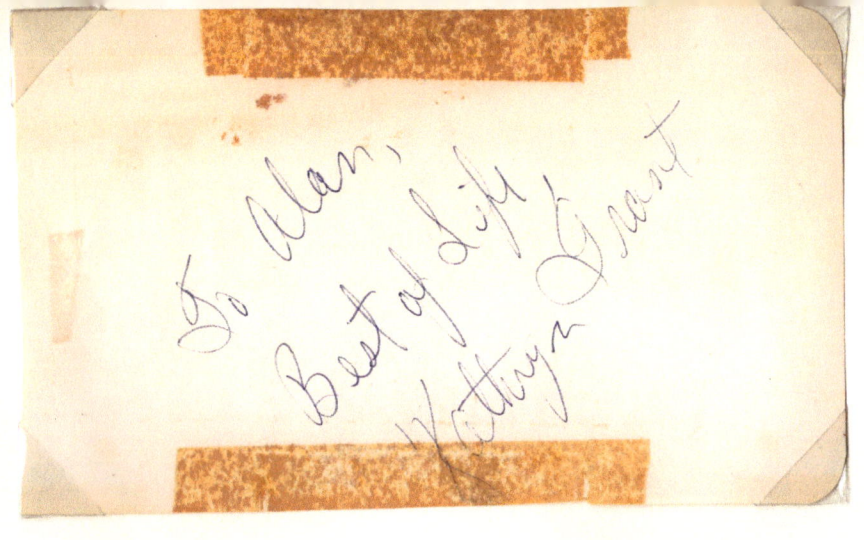
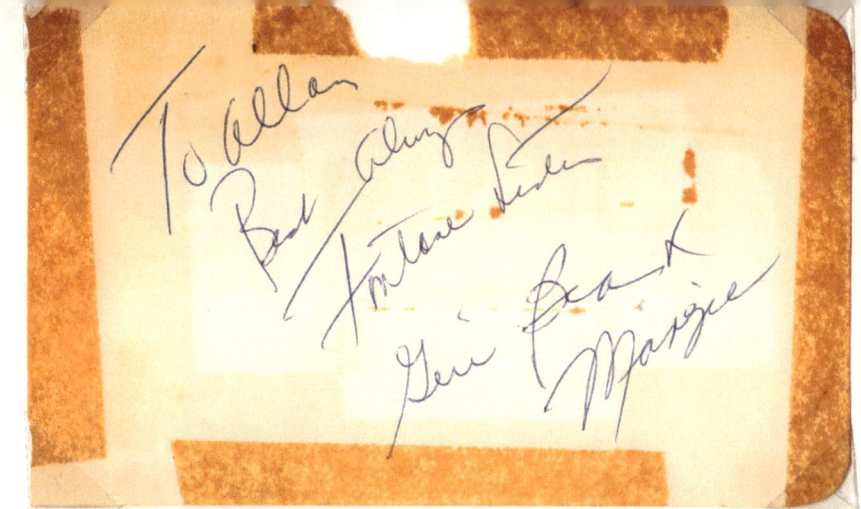
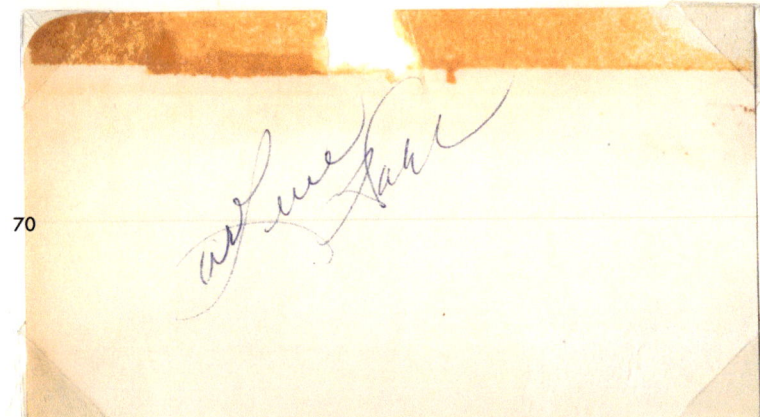
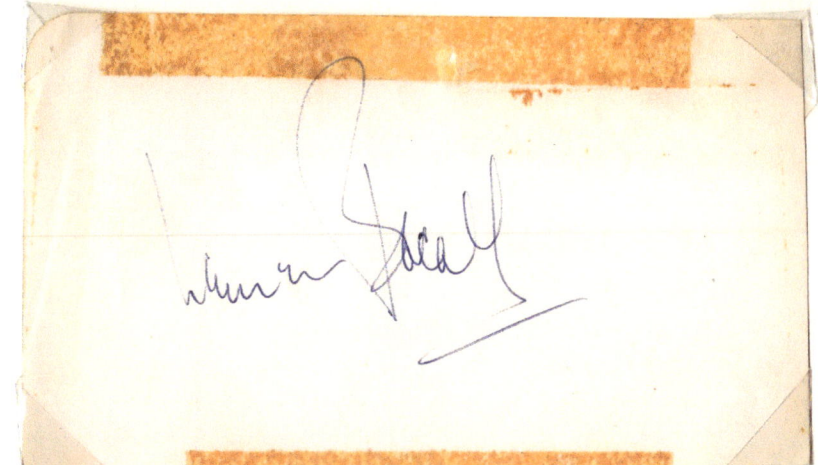
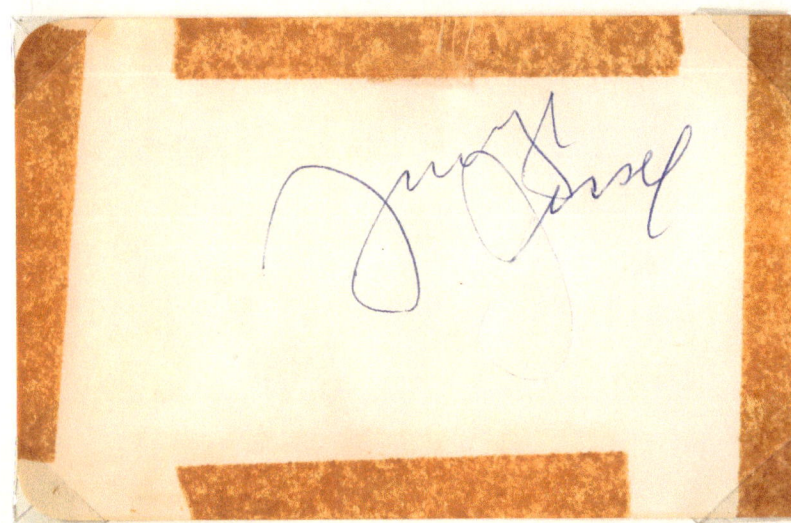
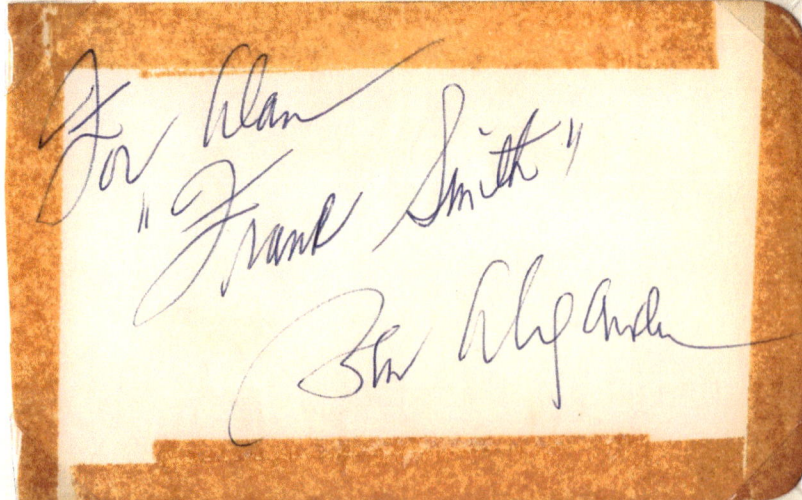

LTCW: Kathryn Grant, Fontane Sisters, Lauren Bacall, "Frank Smith" Ben Alexander, George Jessel, Arlene Dahl

LTCW: Dennis O'Keefe, John Carradine, Margret Leighton, Anna Neagle, Gwen Verdon, Howard St. John

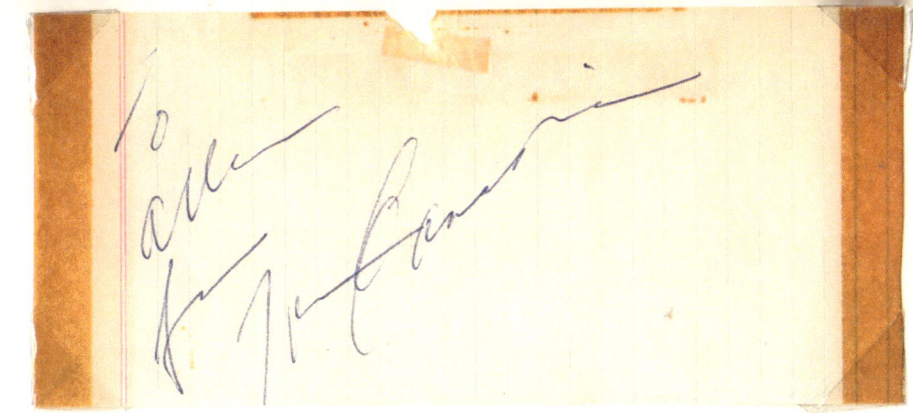
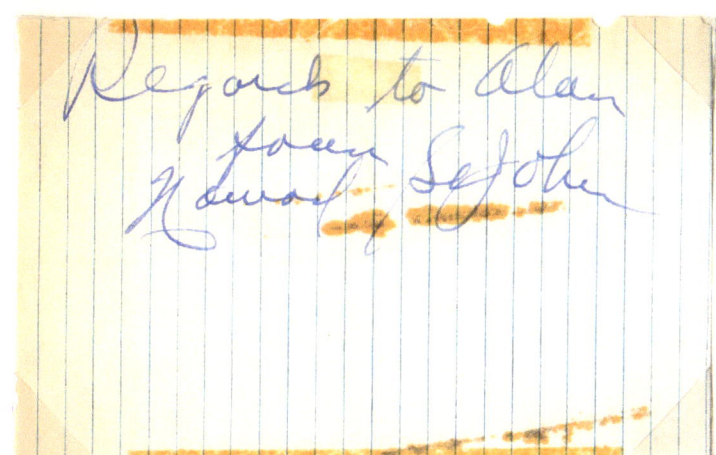
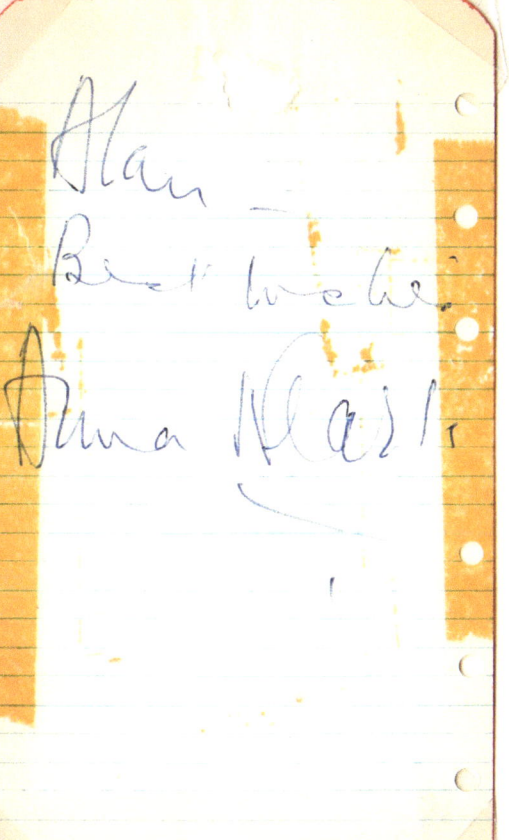
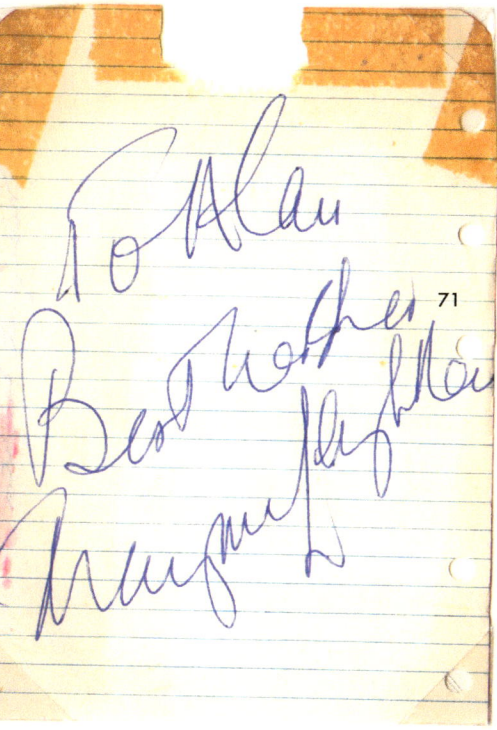

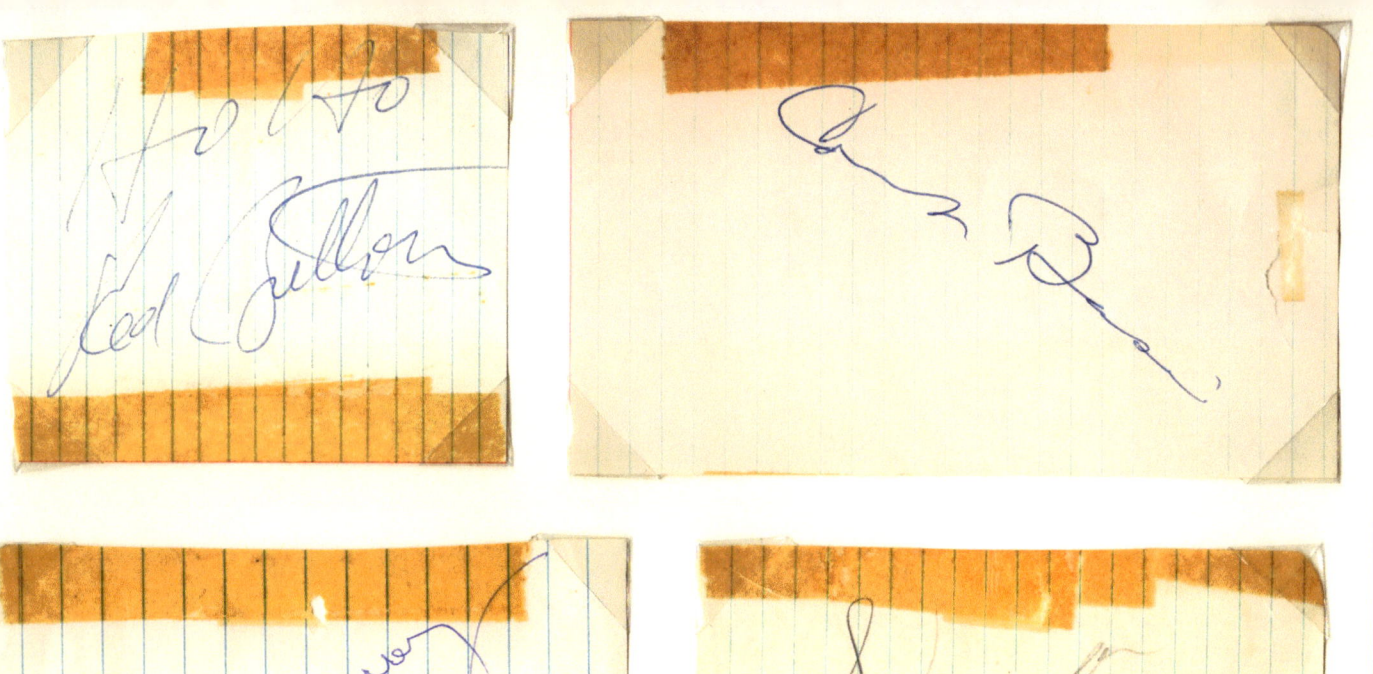
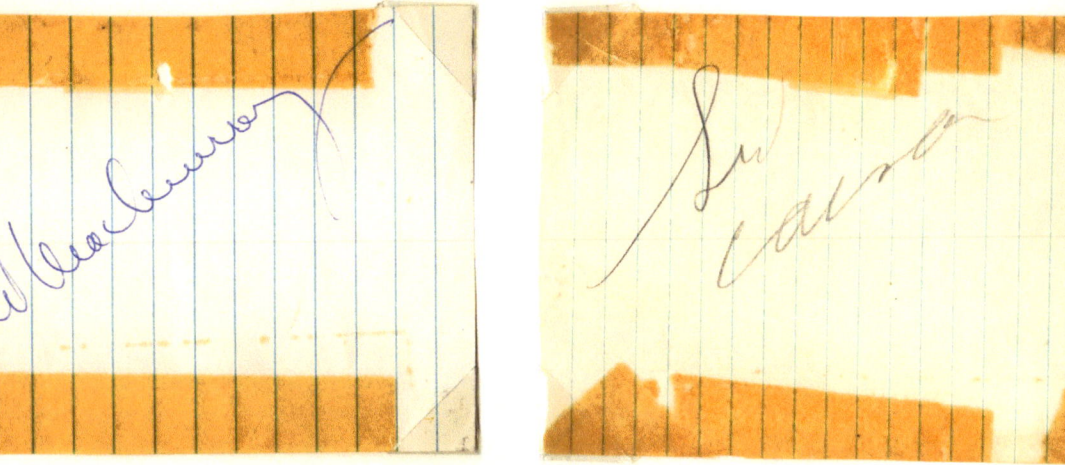
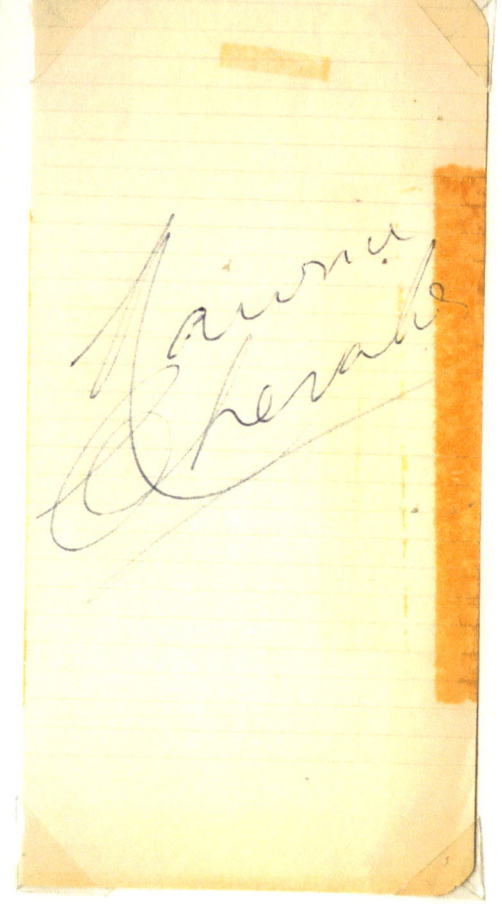
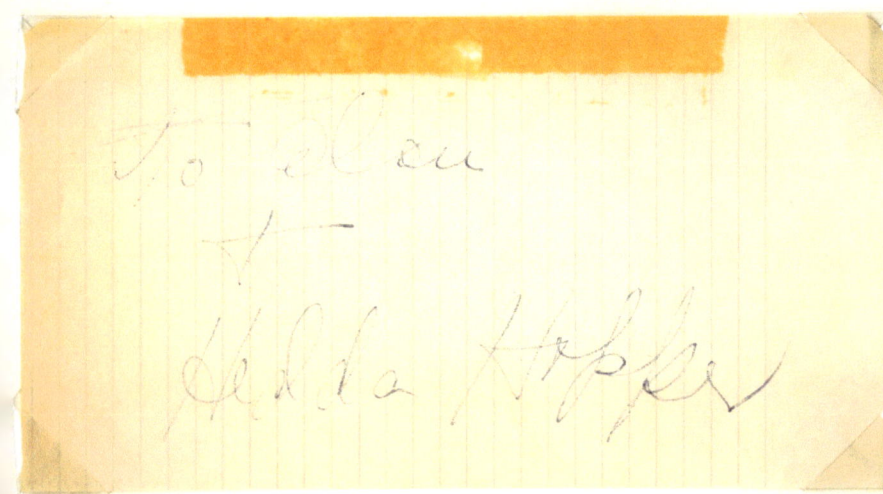

LTCW: Red Buttons, Count Basie, Maurice Chevalier, Elia Kazan, Hedda Hopper, Fred MacMurray, C. Sid Caesar

LTCW: Howard da Silva, Jan Sterling, Georgia Gibbs, Mel Tormé, Dore Schary, Eve Arden, Jimmy Boyd

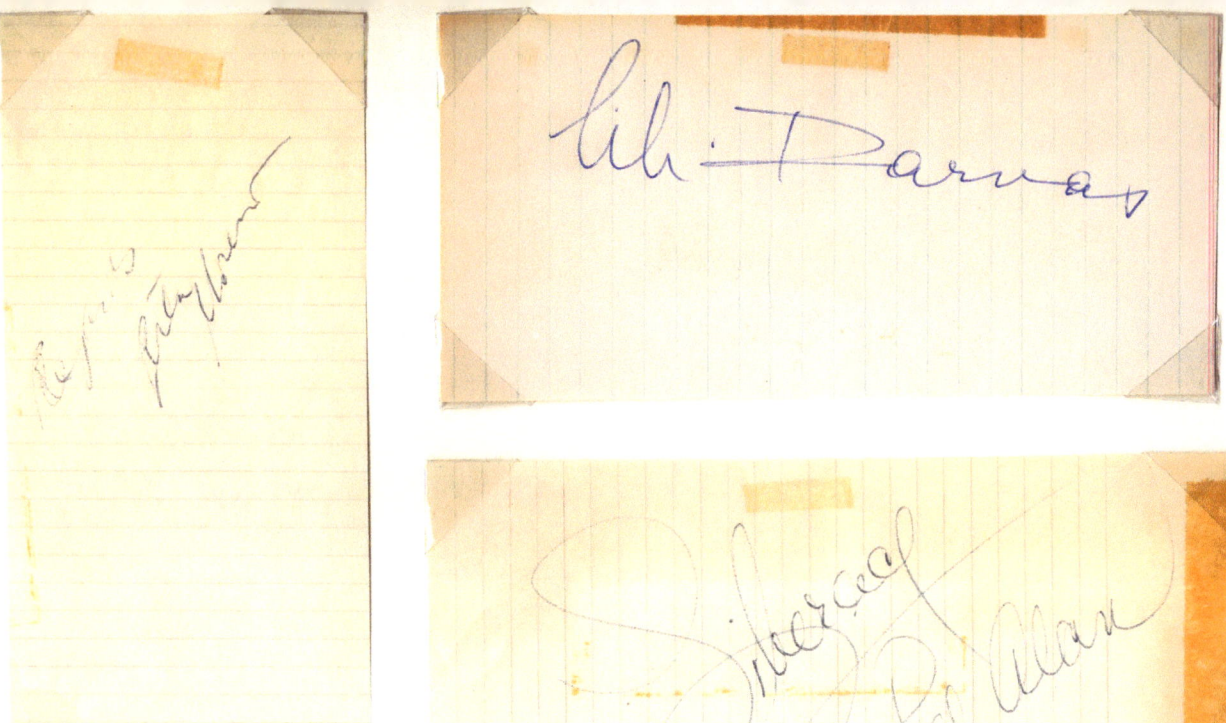
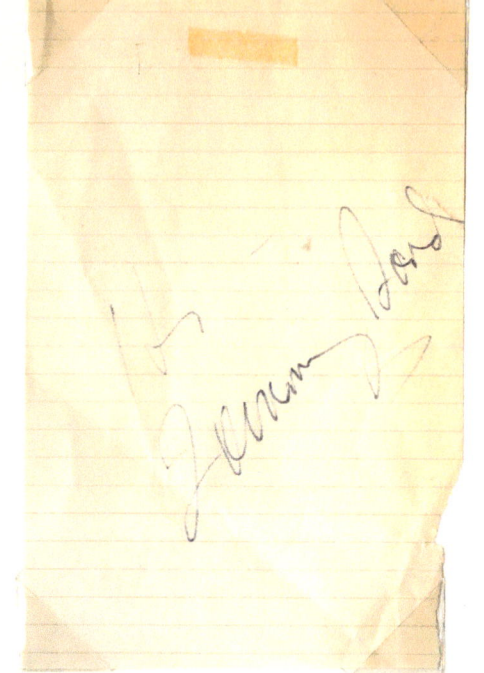
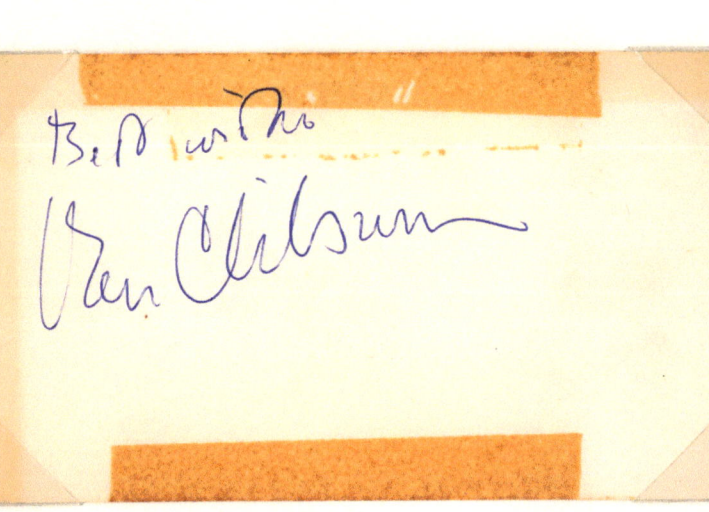
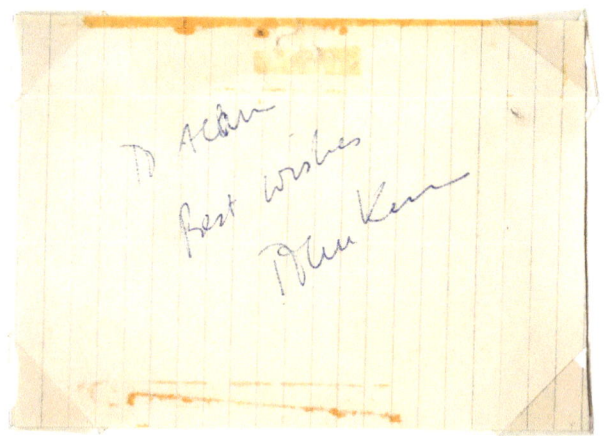

LTCW: Rita Moreno, Lili Darvas, Tommy Sands, Dick York, John Kerr, Van Cliburn, C. Liberace

LTCW: unknown, June Allyson, Milton Berle, Jane Pickens, Cameron Prudhomme, Scott Merrill, Jack Carson

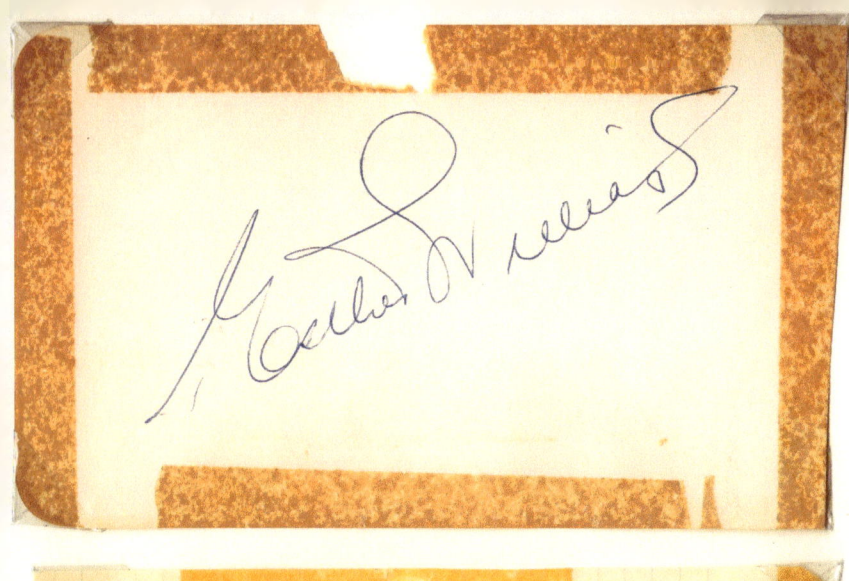
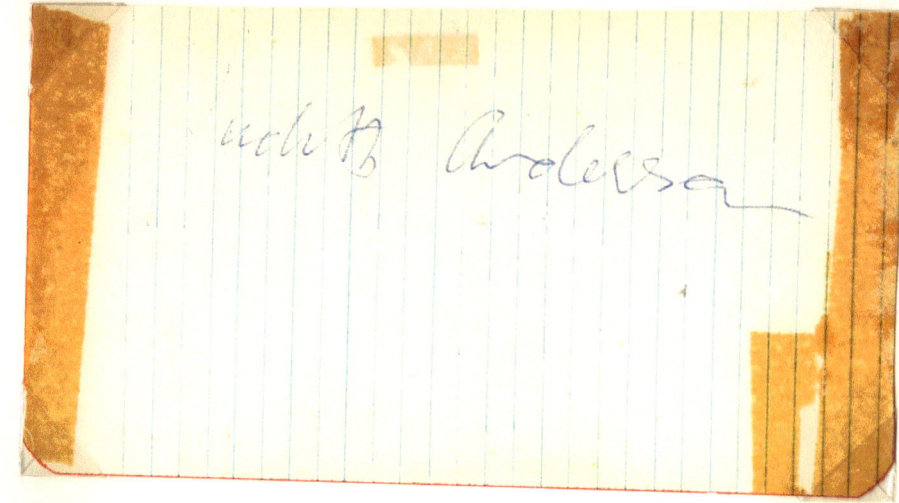
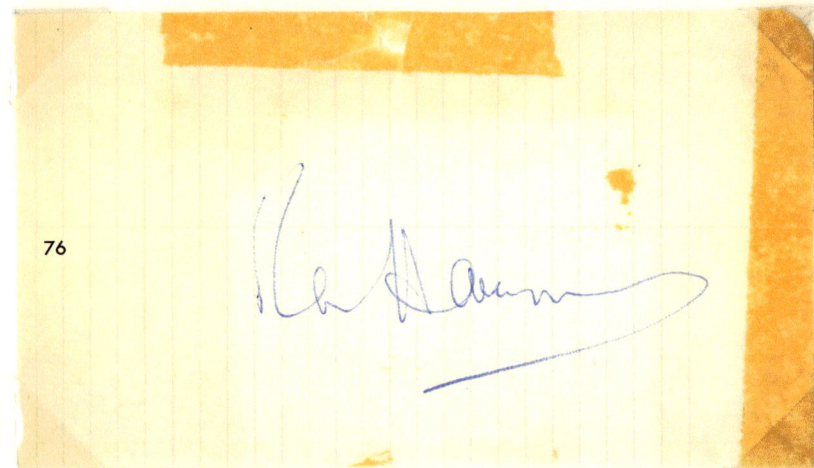
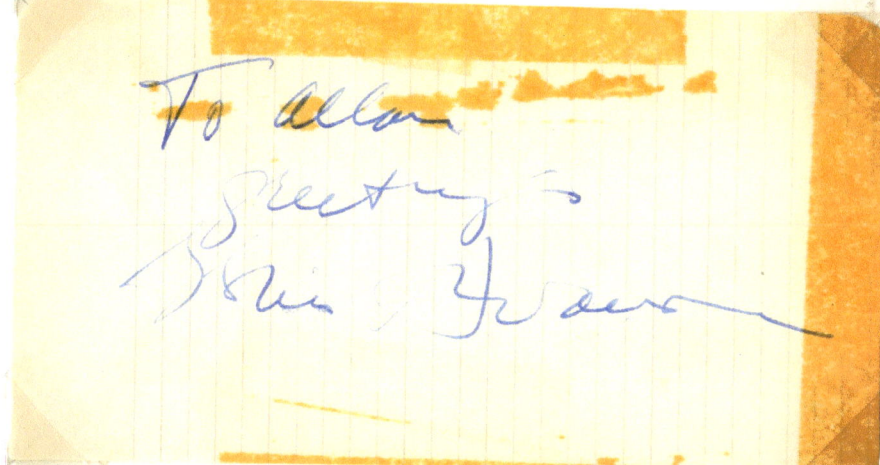
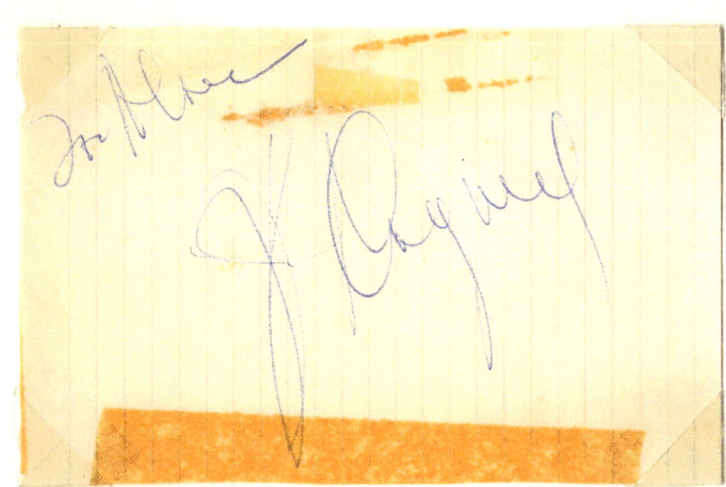
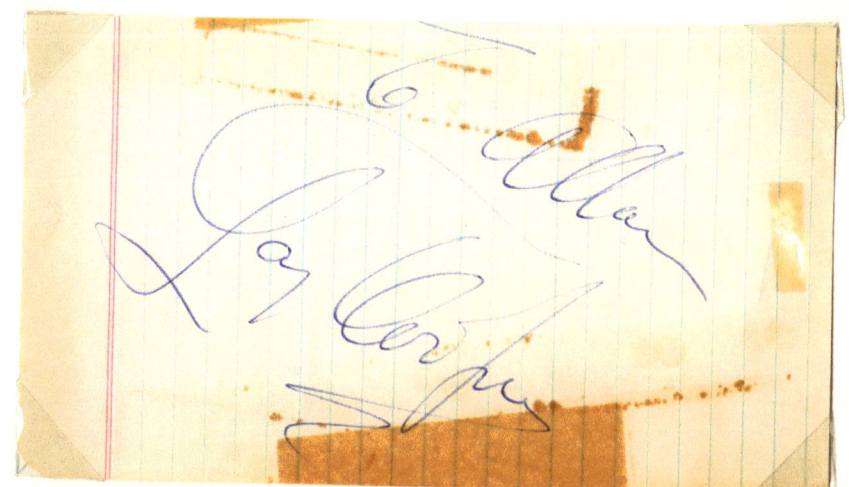

LTCW: Esther Williams, Judith Anderson, Gloria Swanson, Gary Cooper, James Cagney, Rex Harrison

LTCW: Phyllis Thaxter, Morey Amsterdam, Timmy Everett, Magda Gabor, Frederick Loewe, Phyllis McGuire, Scott Forbes, C. Barney Ross

Phyllis Thaxter

To Allan
[Morey Amsterdam]

Thank you
Timmy Everett

To Alan
Barney Ross

Magda Gabor

Hi Alan!
Love
Scott Forbes

To Allan
Sincerely
Phyllis McGuire

To Allen
Frederick Loewe

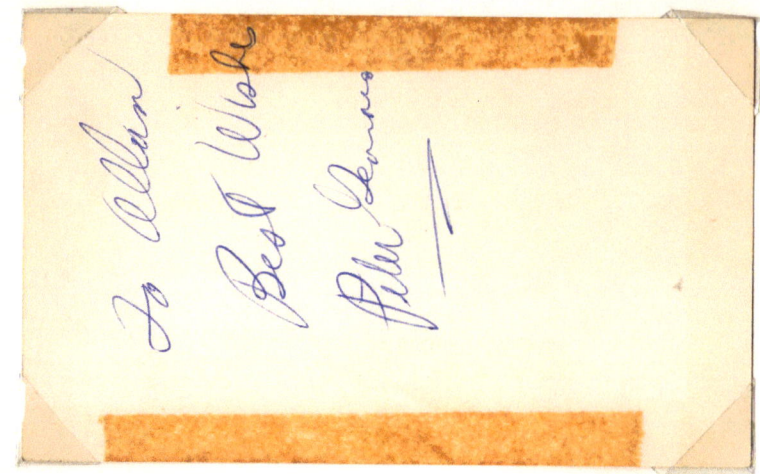

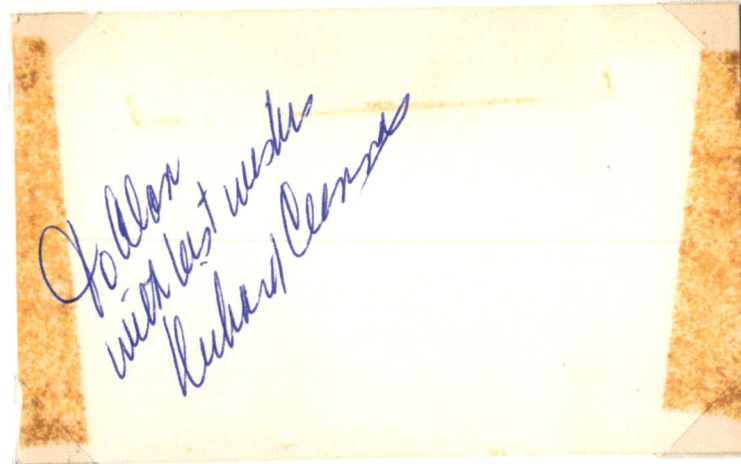

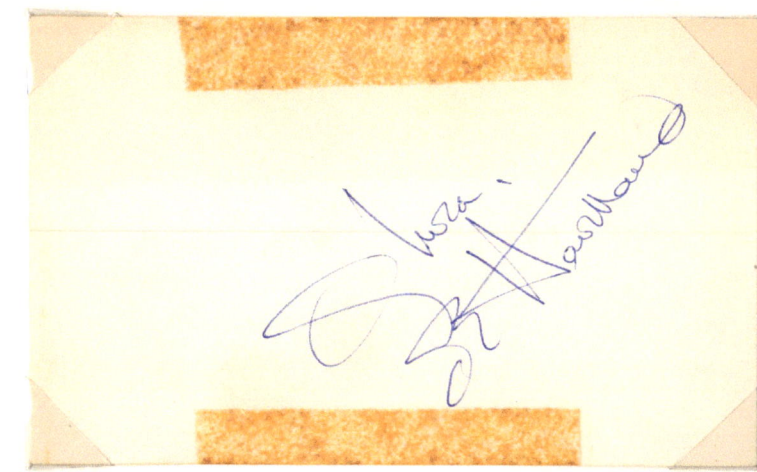

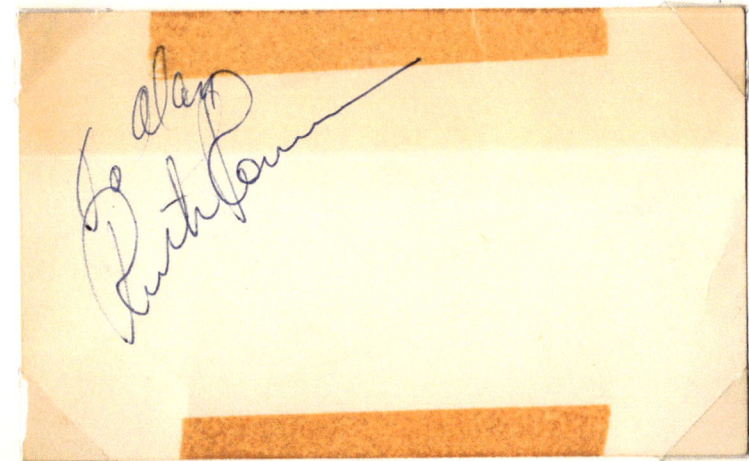

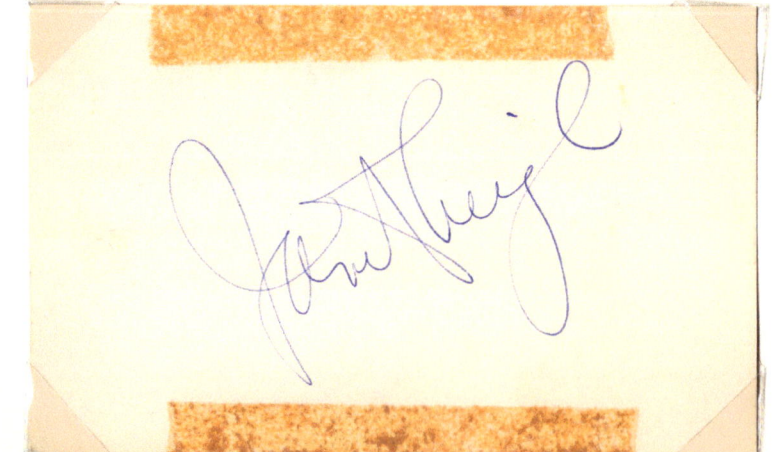

LTCW: Theo Bikel, Peter Gennaro, Olivia De Havilland, Janet Leigh, Ruth Roman, Richard Crenna

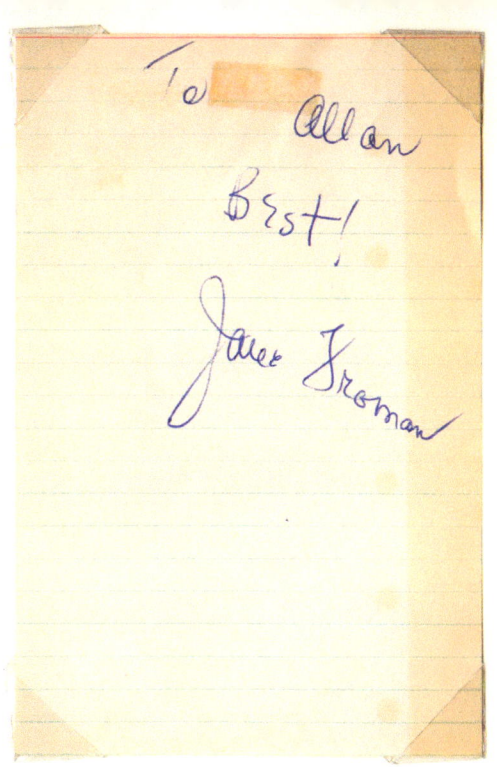
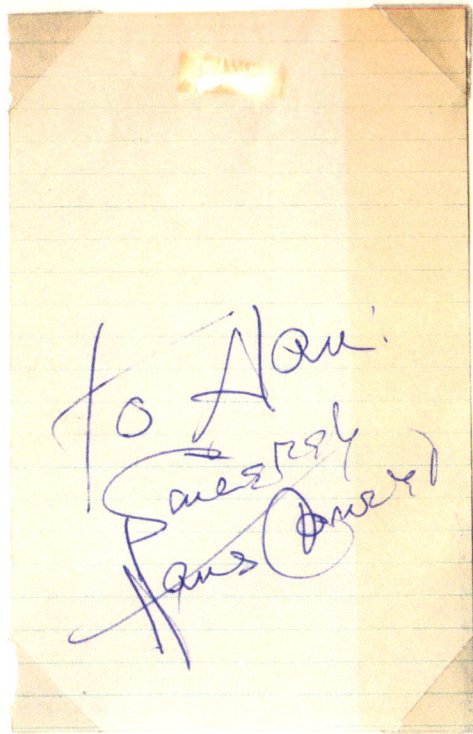

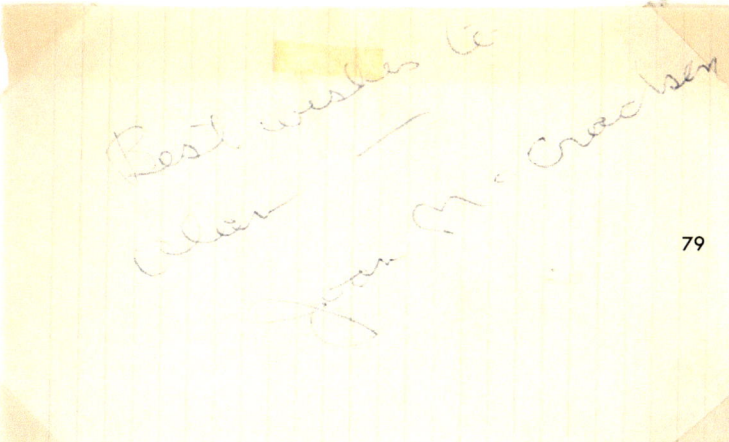
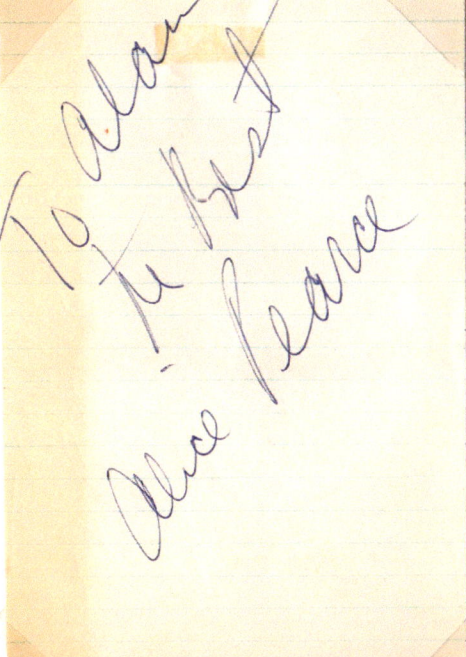

LTCW: Jane Froman, Hans Conreid, Albert Dekker, Joan McCracken, Jane Wyman, Jack Parr, Alice Pearce

LTCW: Kay Kendall, Adolf Green, Jayne Meadows, Toni Arden, Carl Reiner, Don Ameche, Orson Bean, Larry Parkes, C. Ken Carson

LTCW: Diana Dors, Vivian Blaine, Sally Ann Howes, Karl Malden, Clint Kimbrough, James MacArthur, Dan Rowan & Dick Martin, C. Lee Strasburg

81

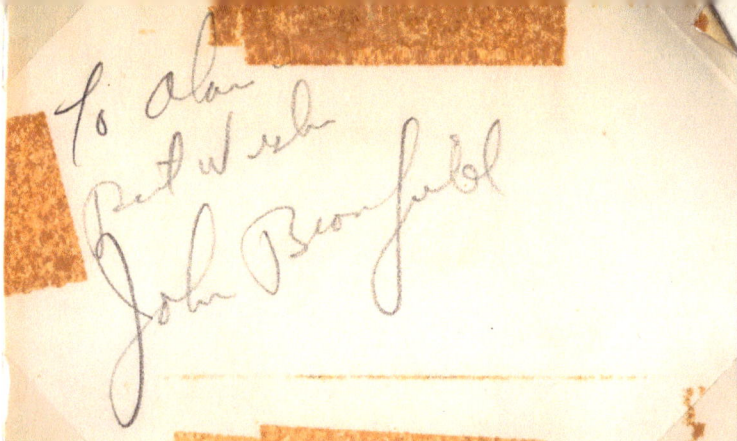
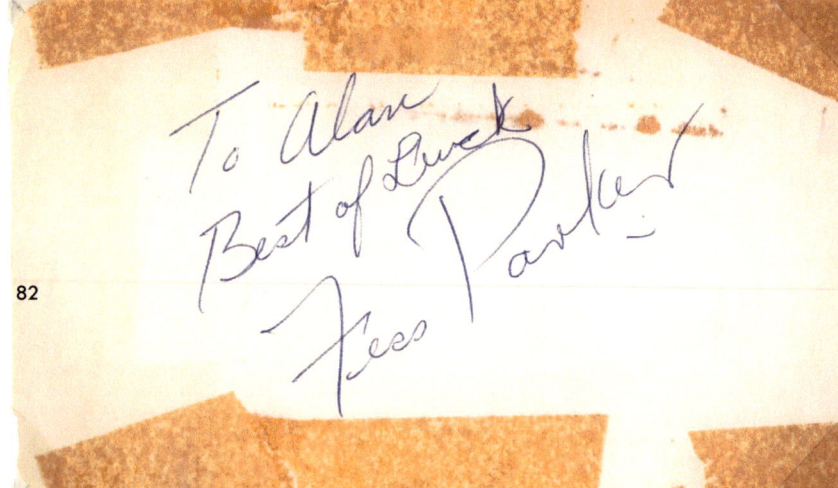

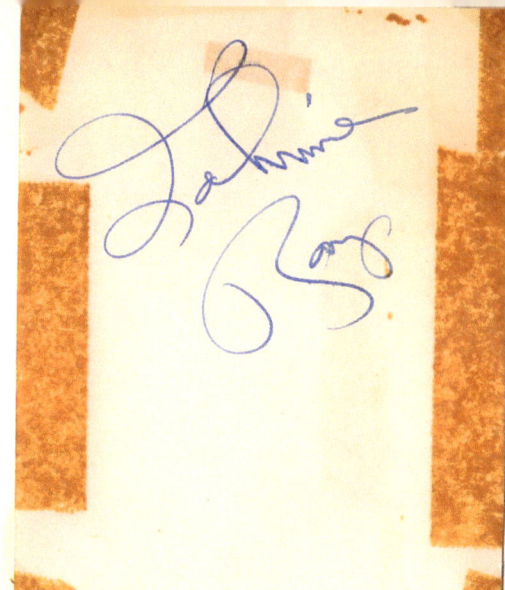

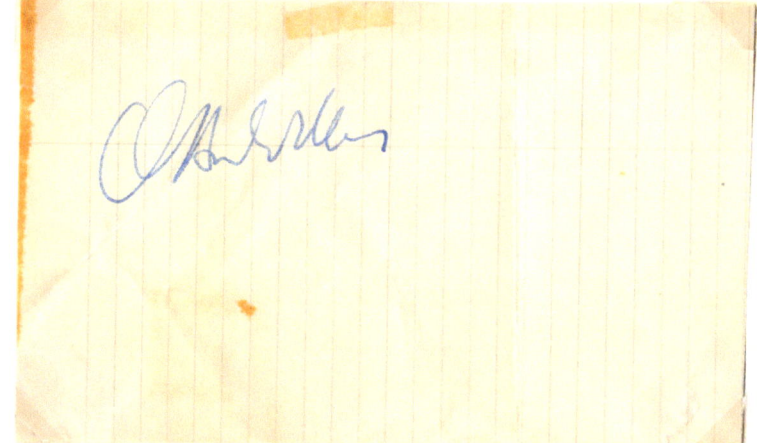
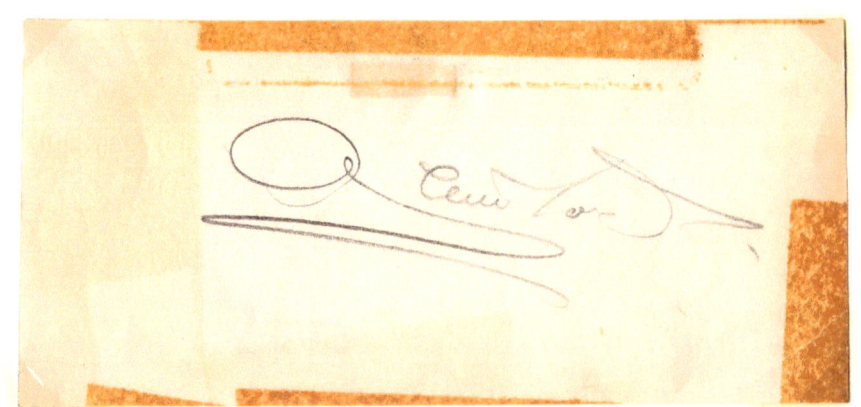

LTCW: John Bromfield, Johnnie Ray, Pat Carroll, Orson Wells, Glenn Ford, Sammy Davis Jr., Fess Parker

LTCW: Jane Powell, George Peppard, Ilka Chase, Dan Dailly, Gary Crosby, Susan Kohner, Paulette Goddard, Eddie Hodges

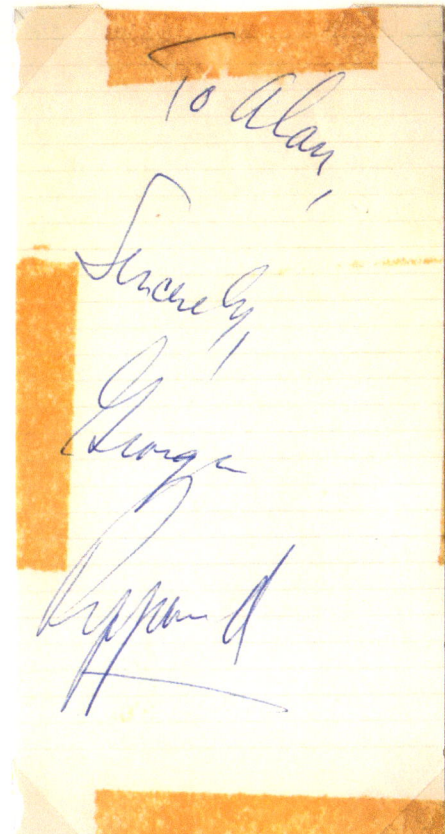

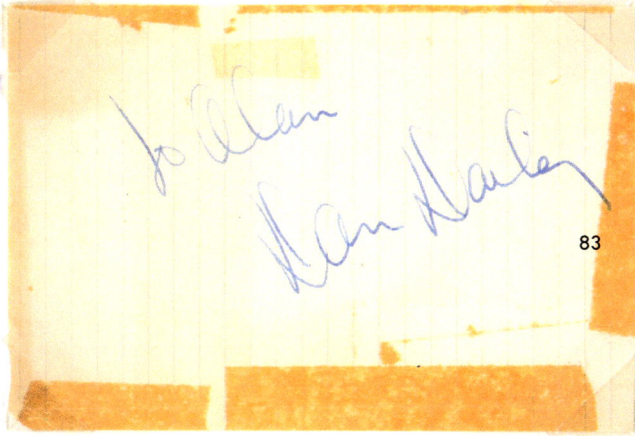
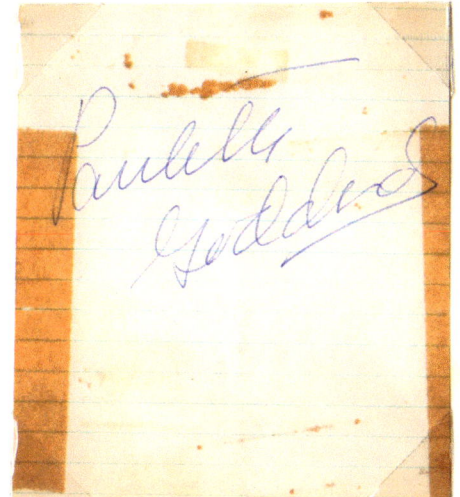

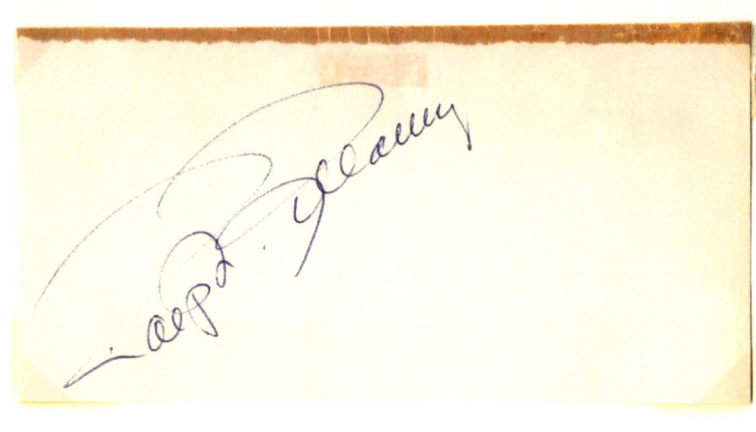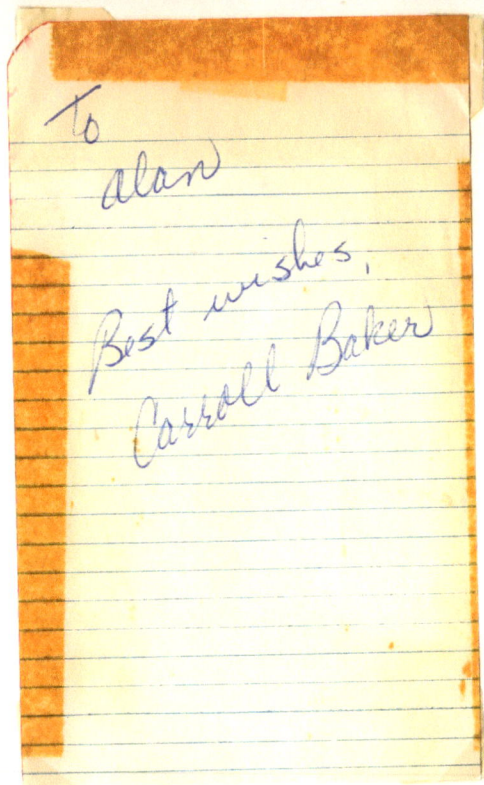

LTCW: Ralph Bellamy, Carroll Baker, Hume Cronyn, Jimmy Durante, Mel Ferrer, Gale Gordon, Ben Hecht

LTCW: Betty Field, Brooks West, Joyce Grenfell, Constance Ford, Jerome Cowan, Kathleen Widdows, Betty Furness, C. George Sanders.

To Alan
best wishes
Betty Field

To Alan —
Betty Furness

To Alan
Best wishes
Kathleen Widdows

To Alan
Good Luck
Brooks West

George Sanders

To Alan
Gertrude
Jerome Cowan

Joyce Grenfell

To Alan
Constance Ford

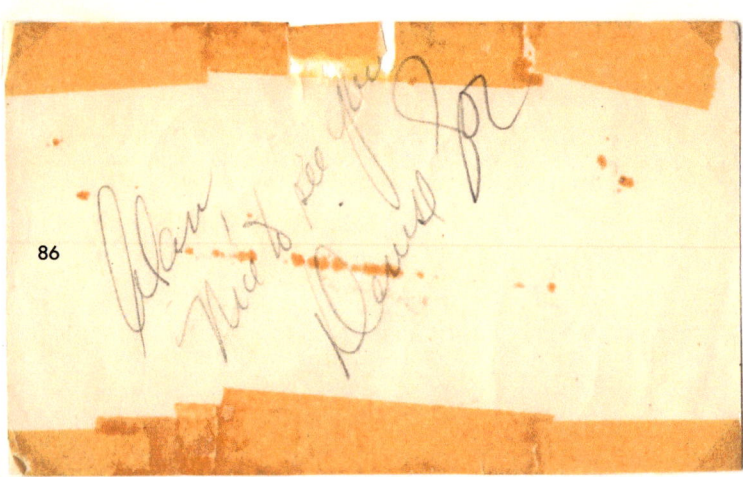
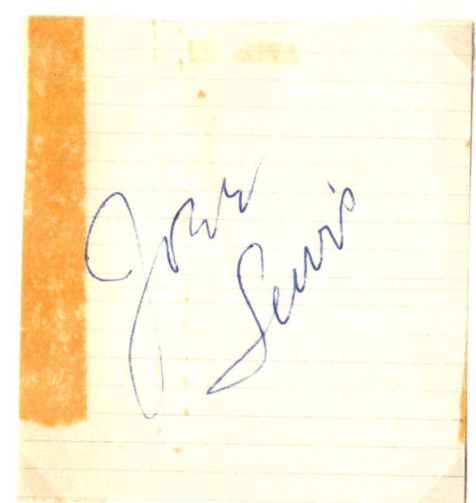

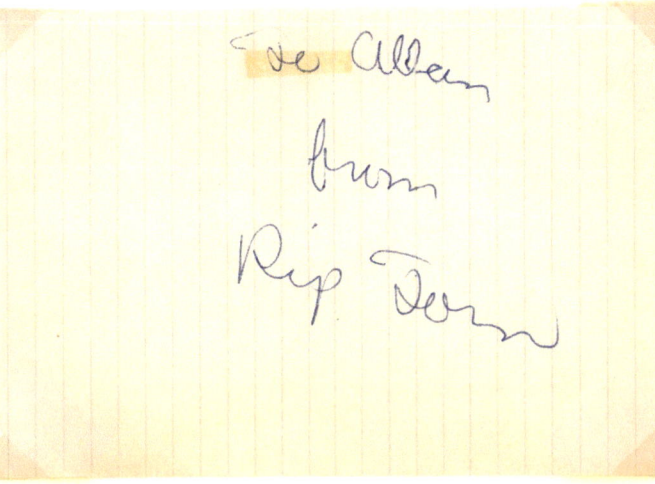

LTCW: Maureen O'Hara, Claudette Colbert, Emmit Kelly, Anita Ekberg, Tyrone Power, Robin Morgan

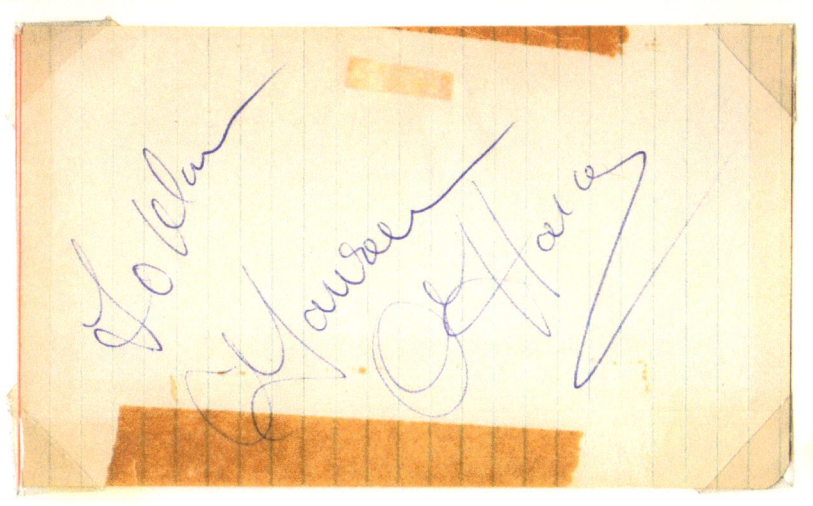
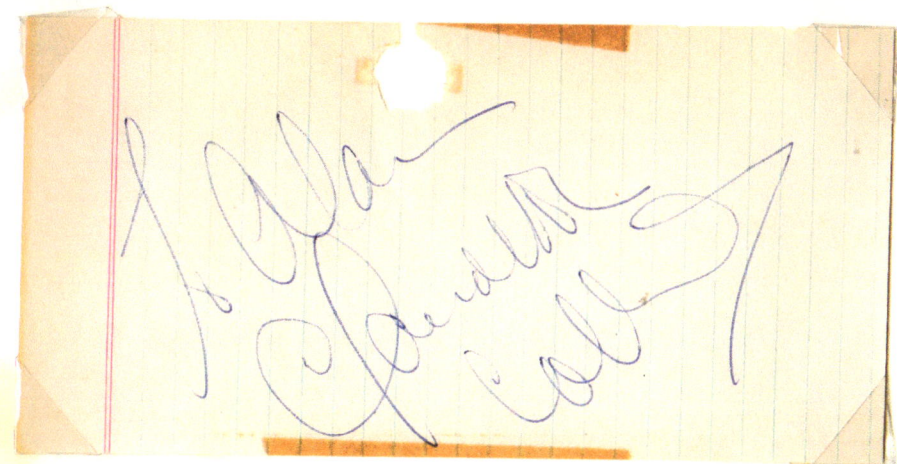

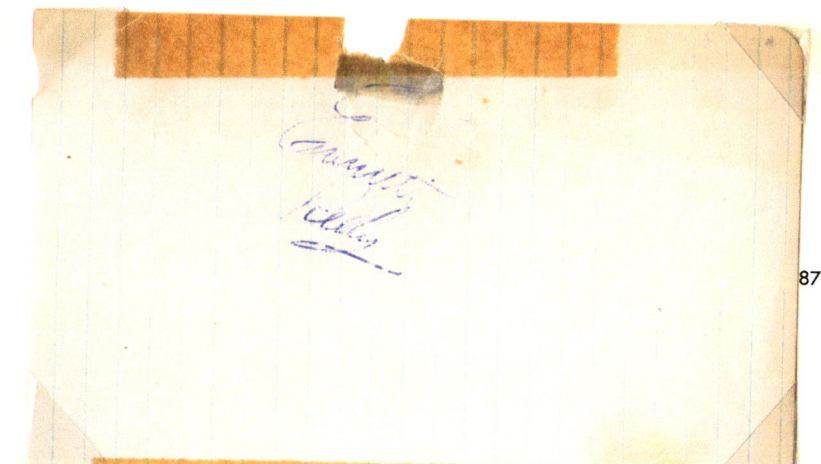
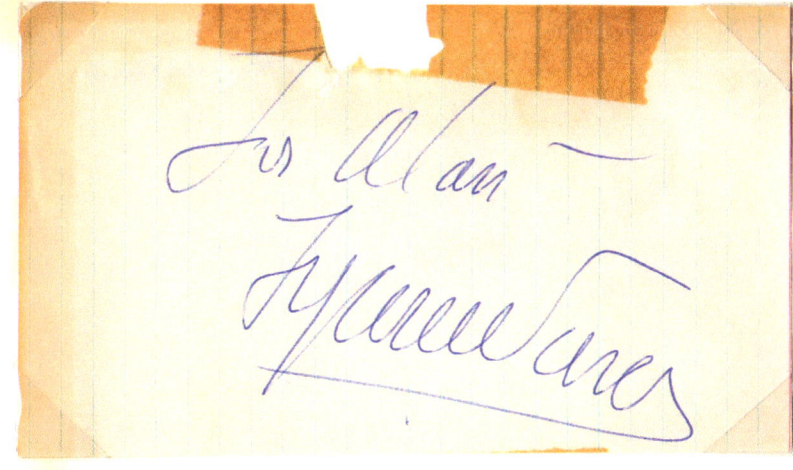
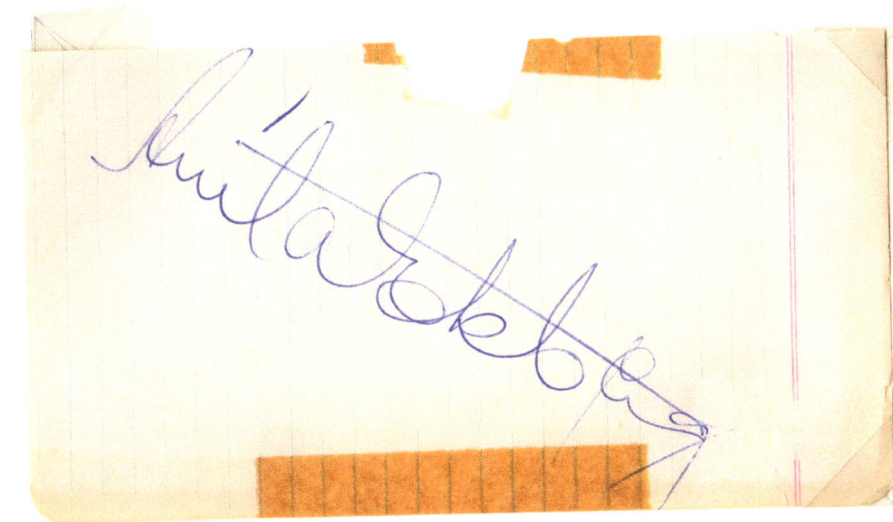

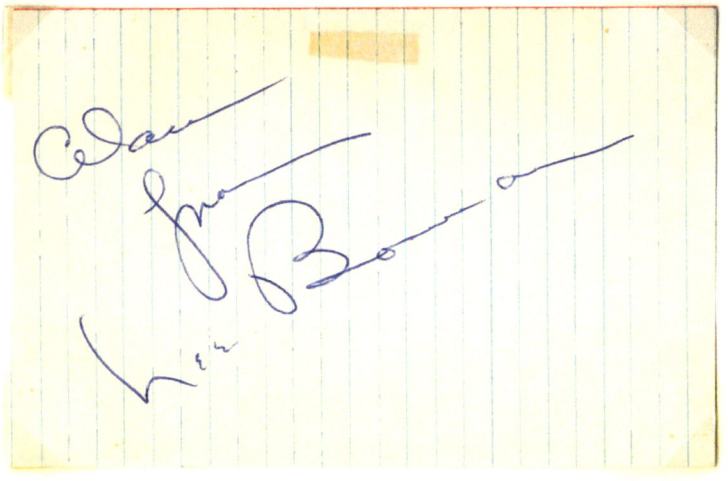

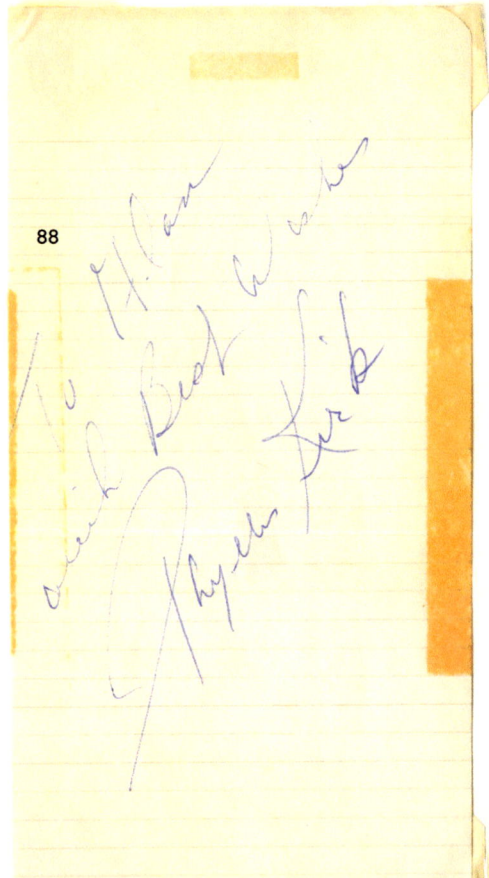

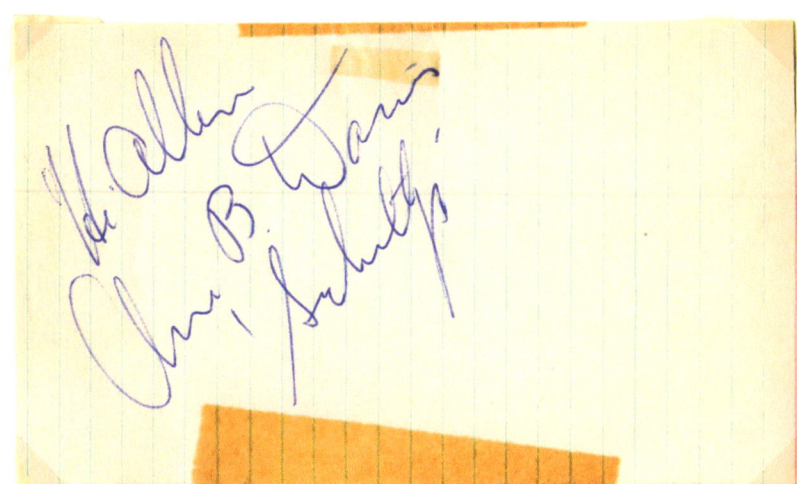

LTCW: Lee Bowman, Dana Andrews, Ann B. Davis, Zizi Jeanmaire, Phyllis Kirk, Patricia Neal

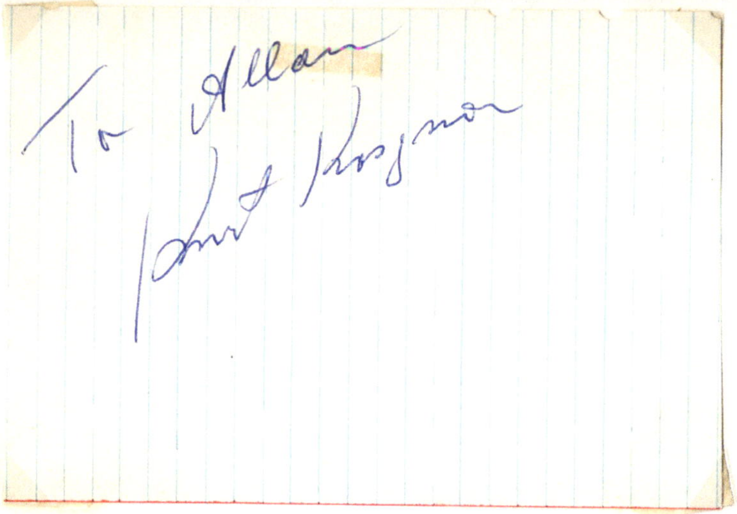

90

To Allan
Kurt Kasner

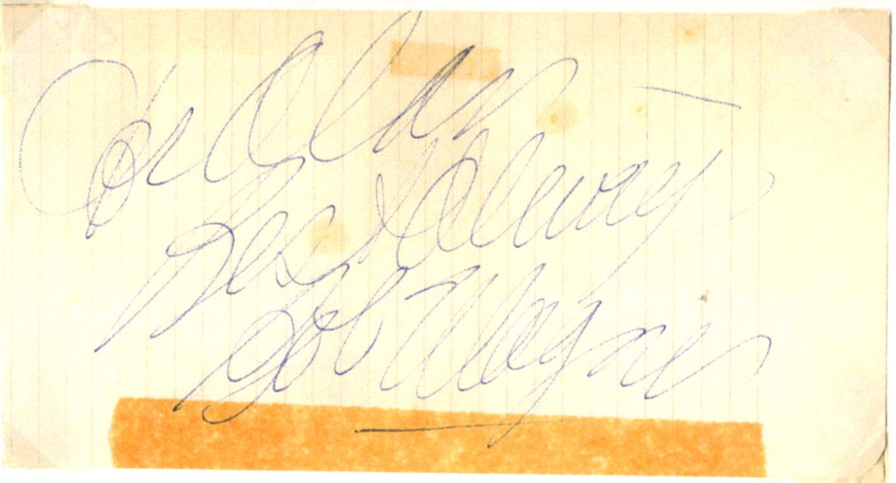

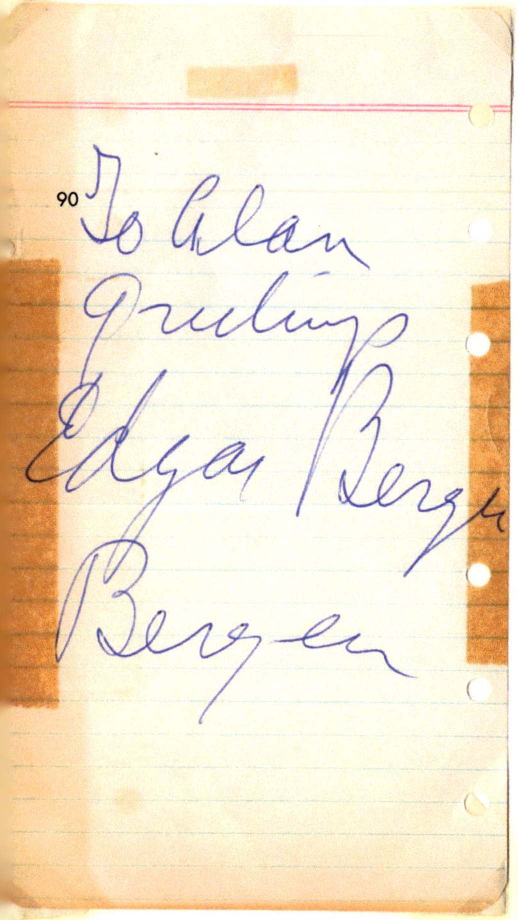

To Allan
Ted Kelloway(?)
Bob Wagner

To Alan
Greetings
Edgar Bergen
Bergen

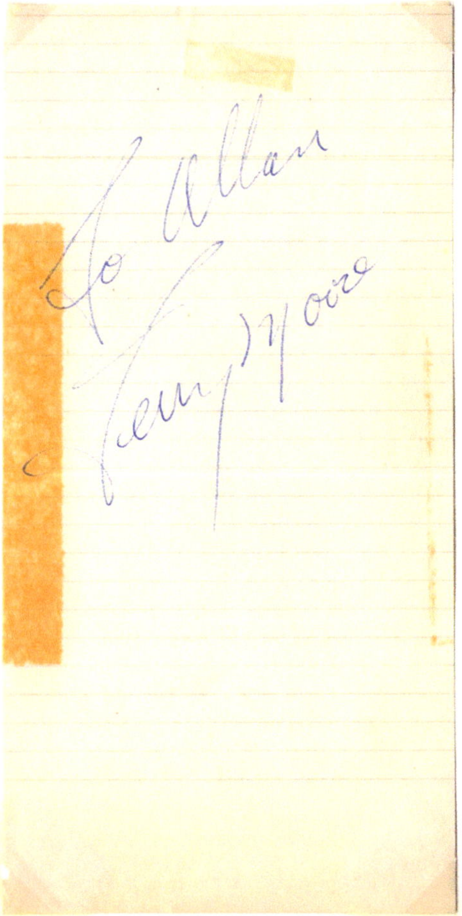

To Allan
Terry Moore

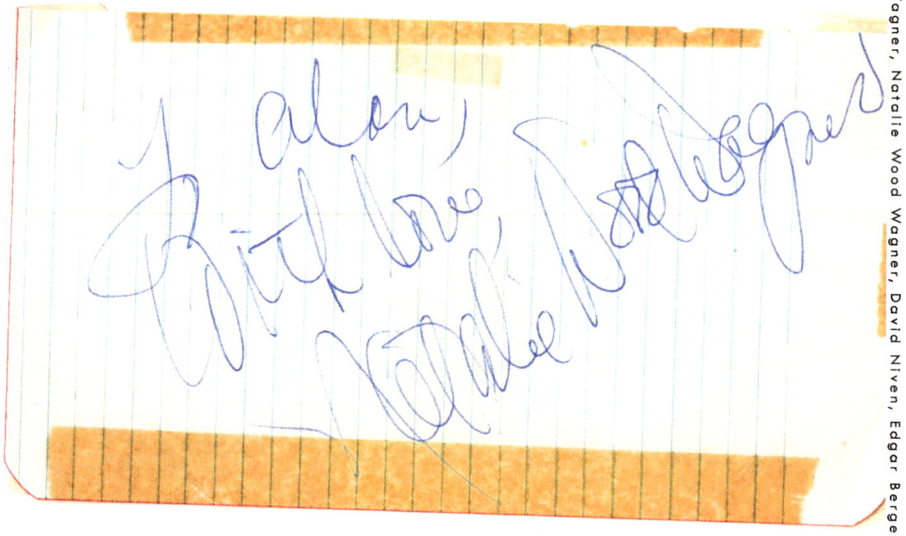

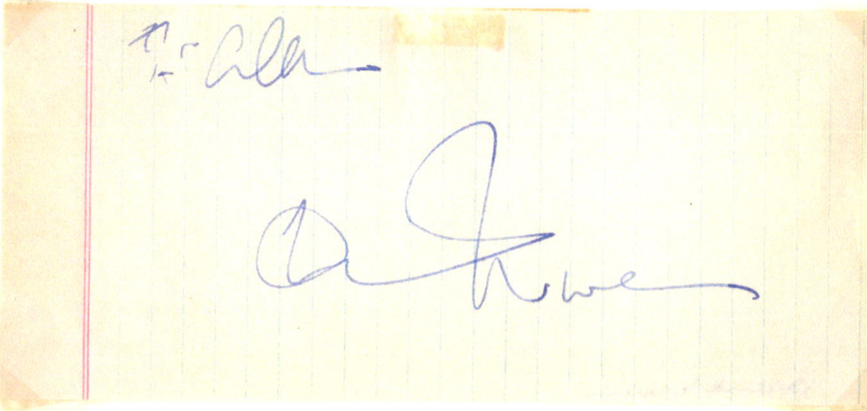

To Alan,
With love
Natalie Wood Wagner

To Alan
David Niven

LTCW: Vera Ralston, Van Heflin, Cesare Romero, Richard Kiley, Scott Brady, Patty McCormack

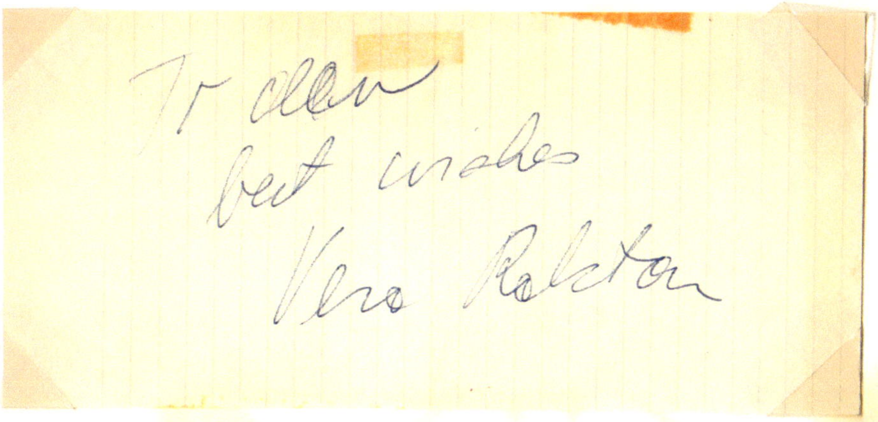

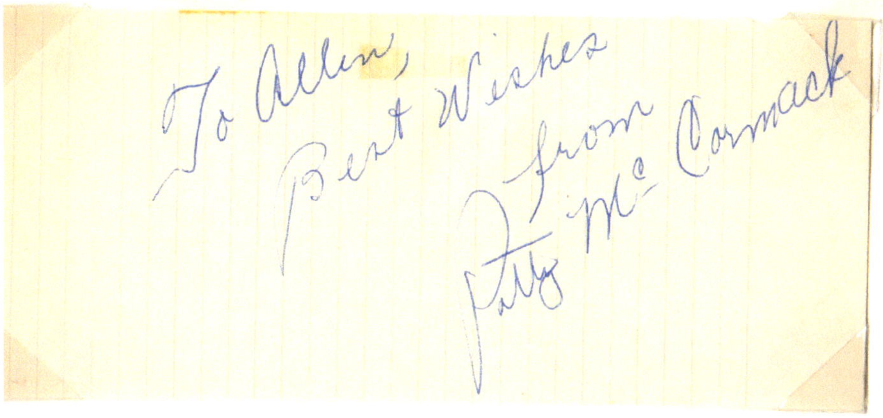

To Allen
best wishes
Vera Ralston

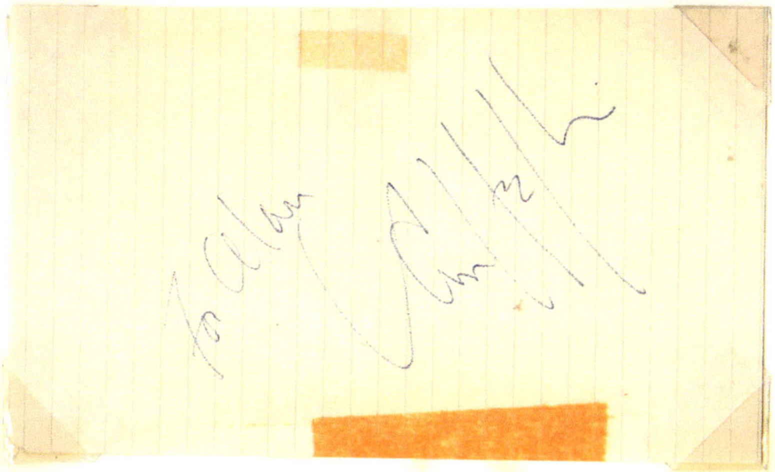

To Alan
Van Heflin

To Allen,
Best Wishes
from
Patty McCormack

To Alan
Best from
Cesar Romero

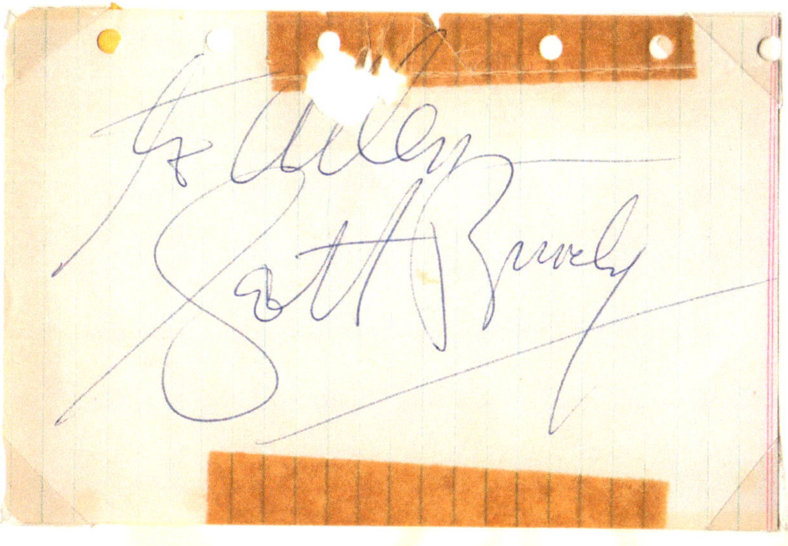

To Allen
Scott Brady

To Alan
Richard Kiley

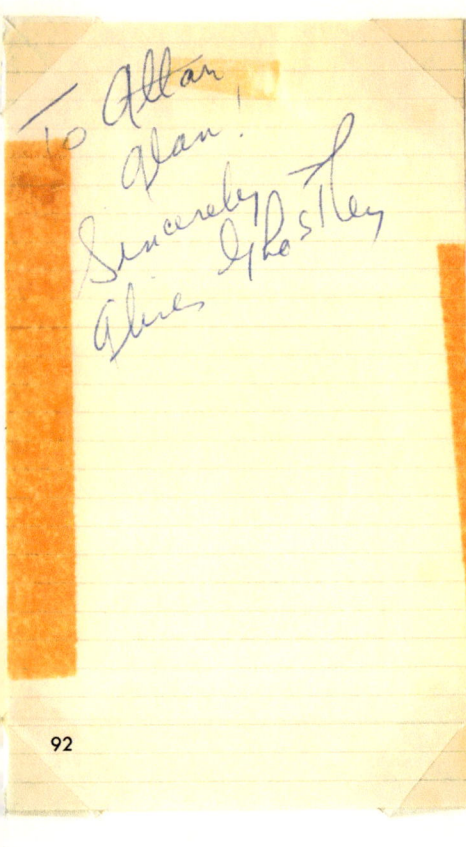
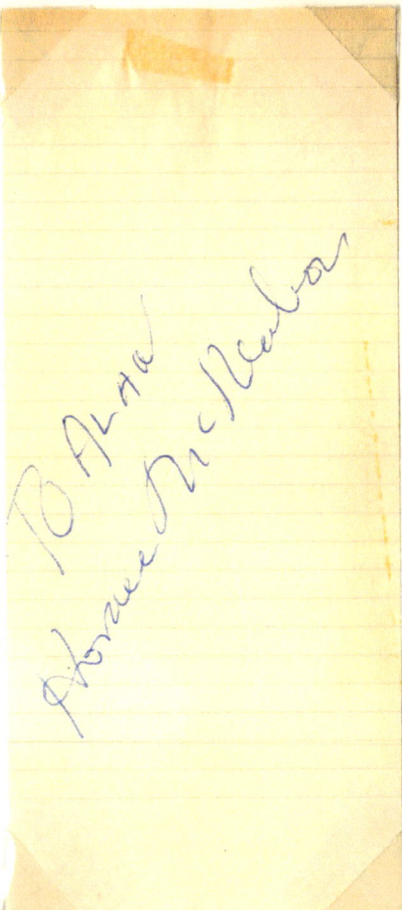

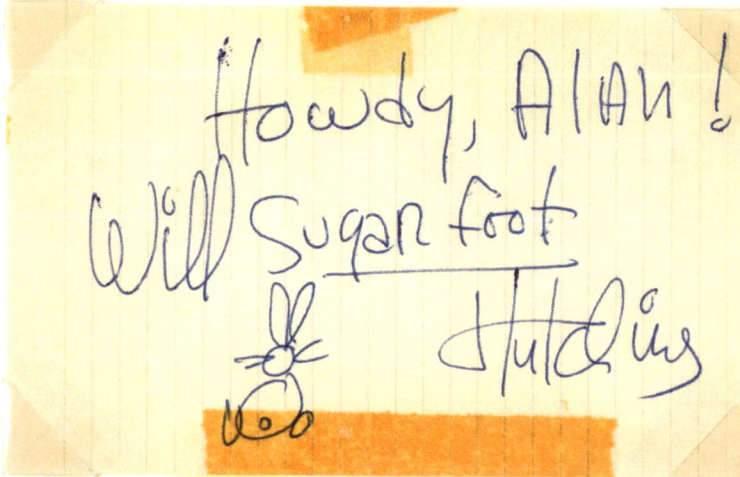

LTCW: Alice Ghostley, Horace McMahon, Dorothy McGuire, Gina Lollobrigida, Sam Levine, Will Hutchins

LTCW: James Whitmore, Linda Christian, Benny Fields & Blossom Seeley, David Wayne, Carol Lawrence, Dane Clark

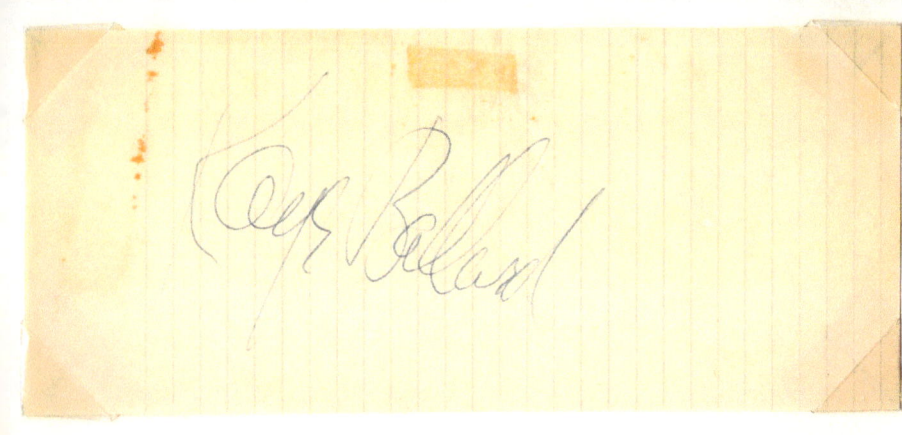

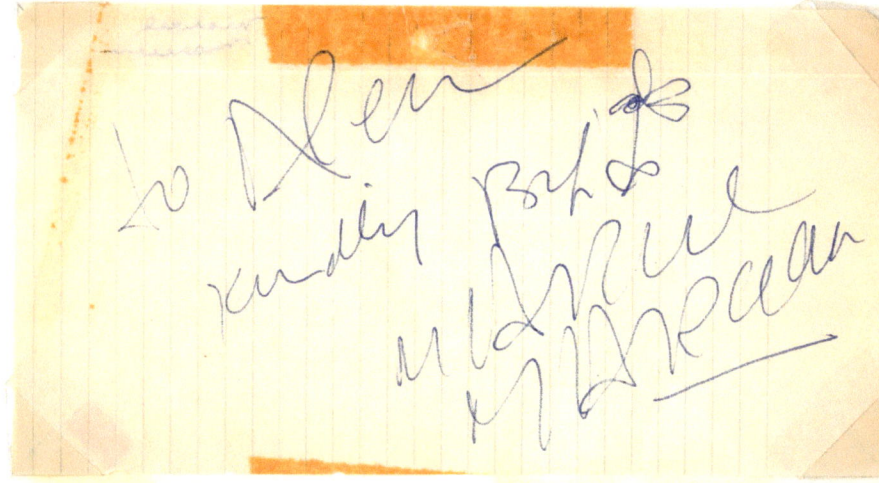

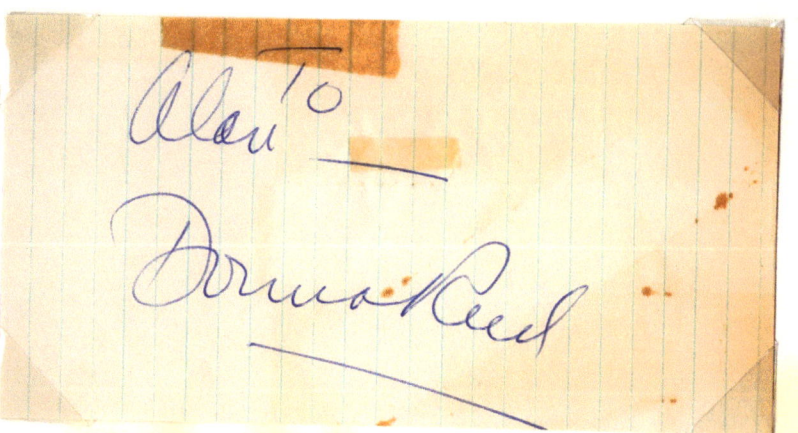

LTCW: Kaye Ballad, Henry Fonda, Donna Reed, Marcel Marceau, Gene Kelly

LTCW: Gloria Vanderbilt, Ralph Meeker, Sidney Poitier, Laurence Olivier, Kevin McCarthy, Julie Andrews, Cathleen Nesbit

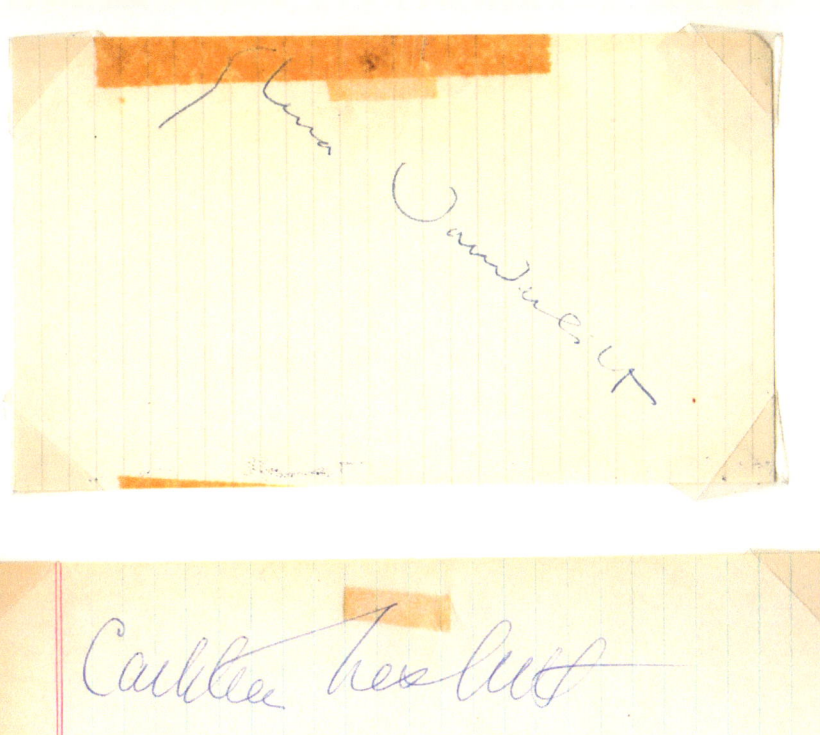
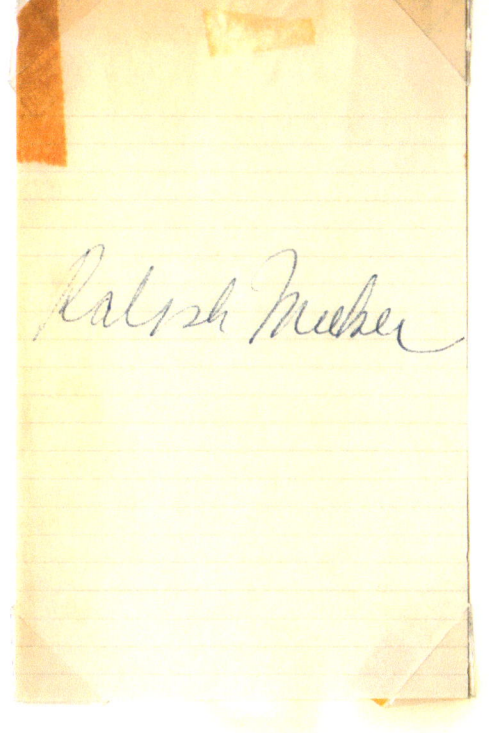
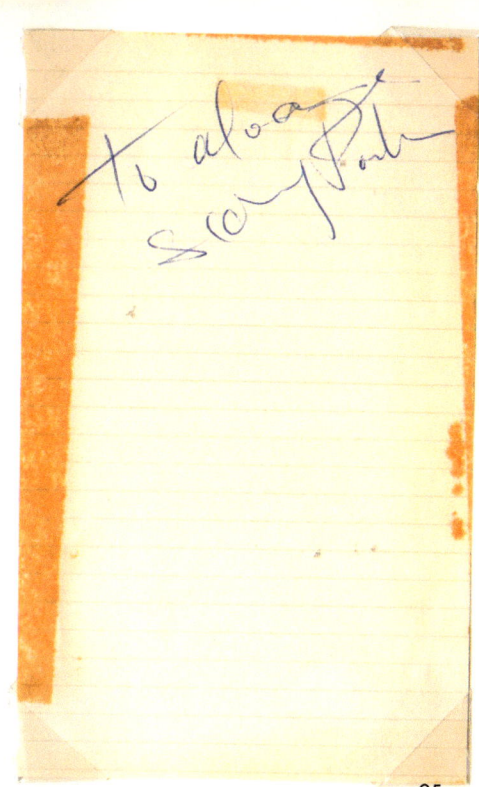

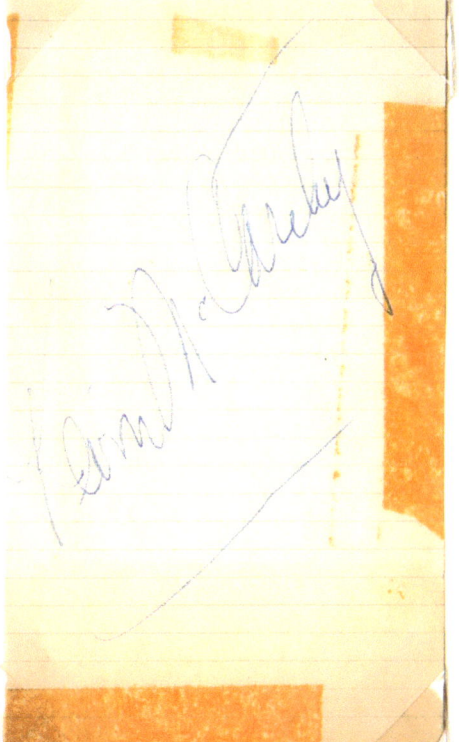
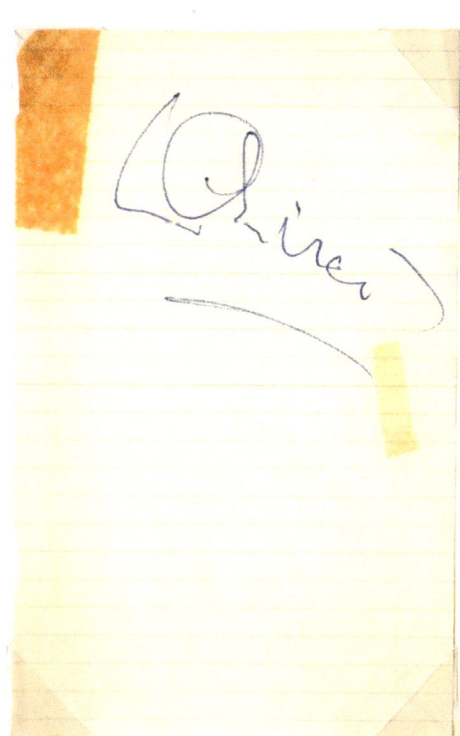

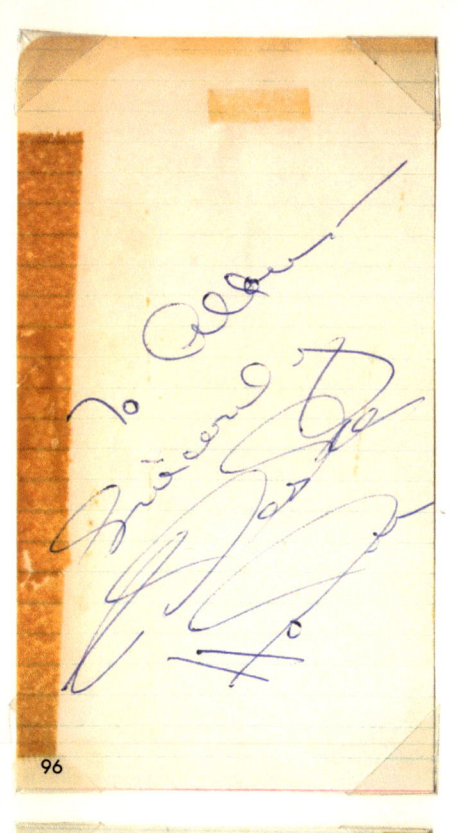
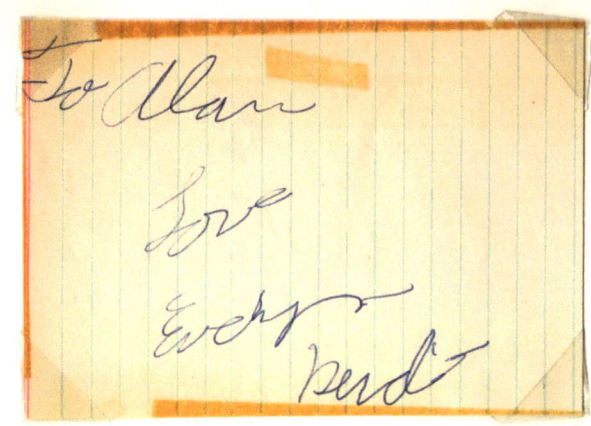

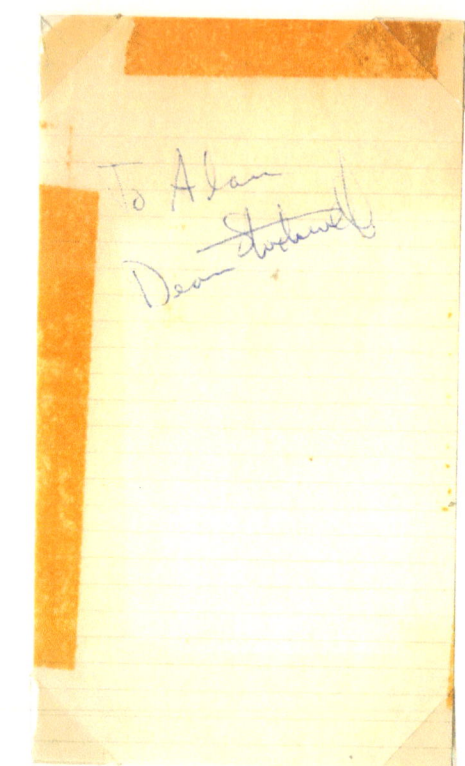
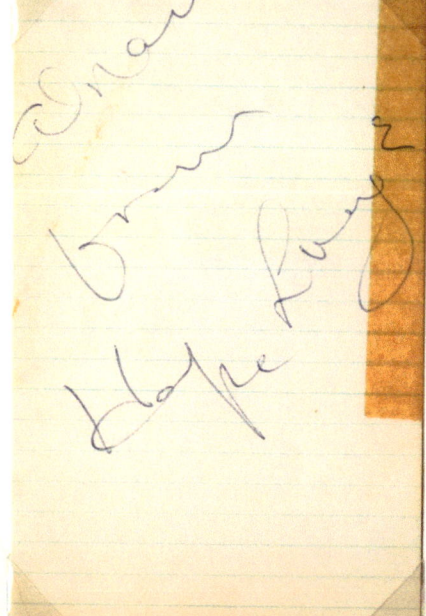

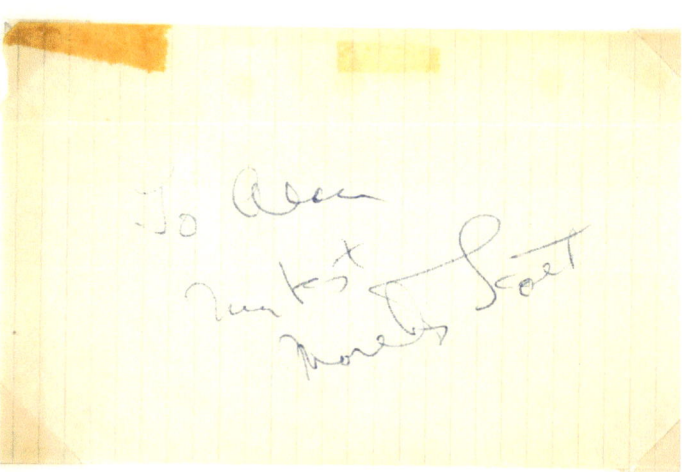

LTCW: Celeste Holm, Evelyn Rudie, Dean Stockwell, Martha Scott, Kirk Douglas, Hope Lange, C. Don Knotts

LTCW: Joanne Woodward, Gene Raymond, Tony Perkins, Anne Baxter, Gertrude Berg, Paul Newman

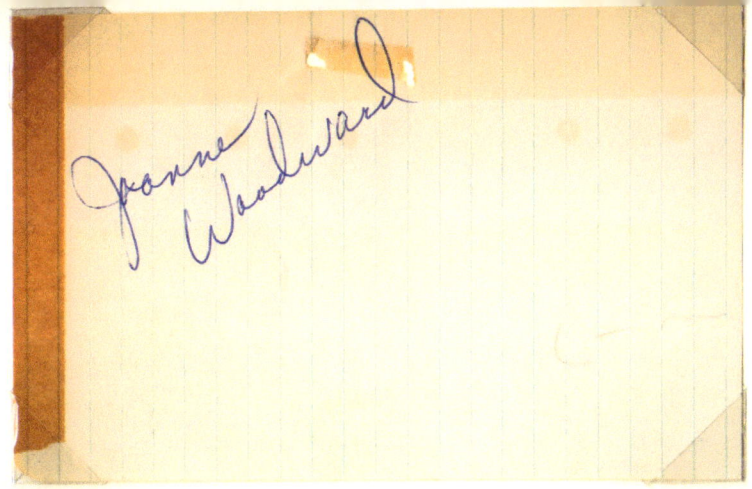
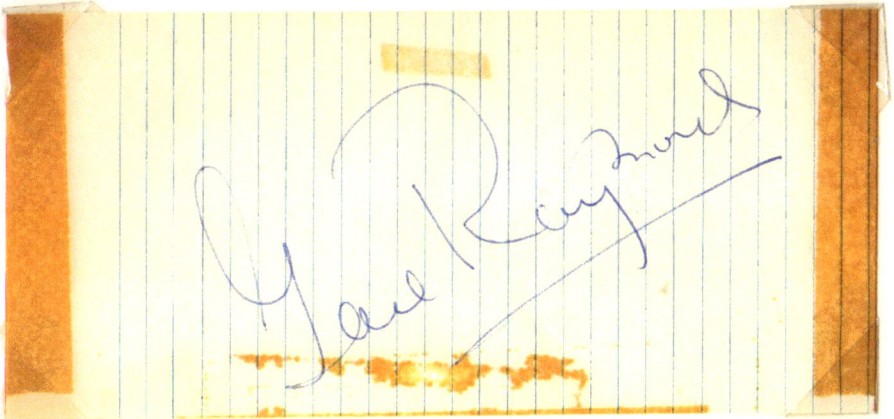
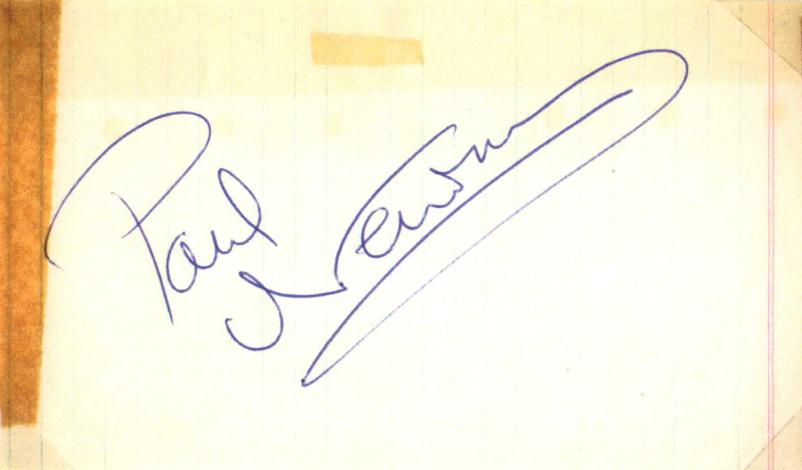
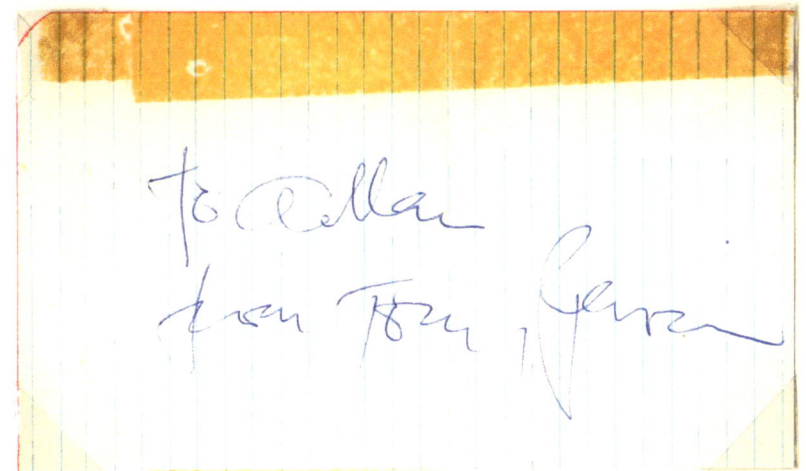
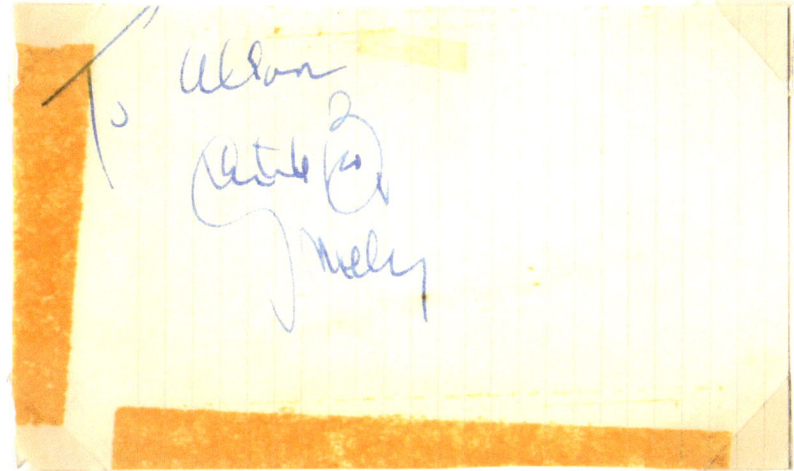

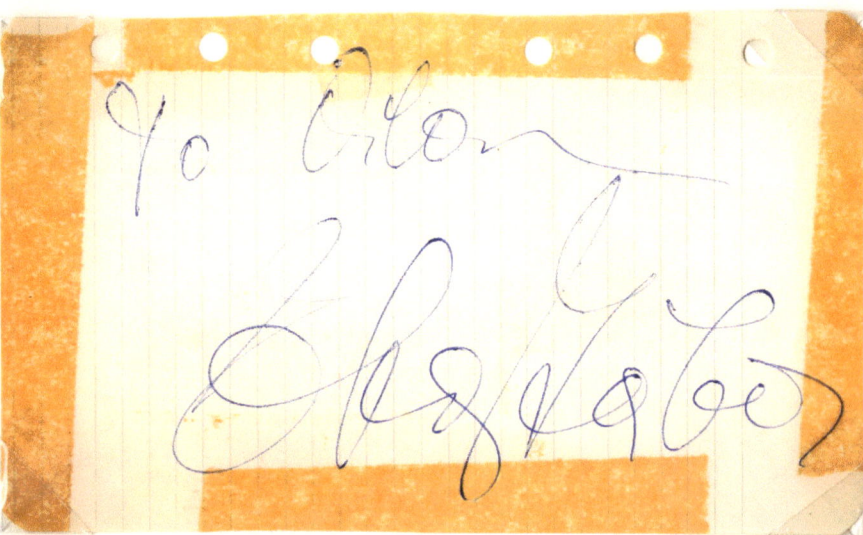
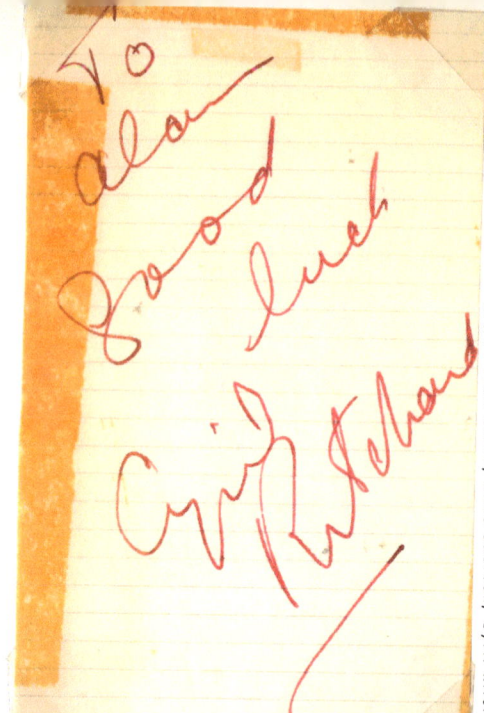
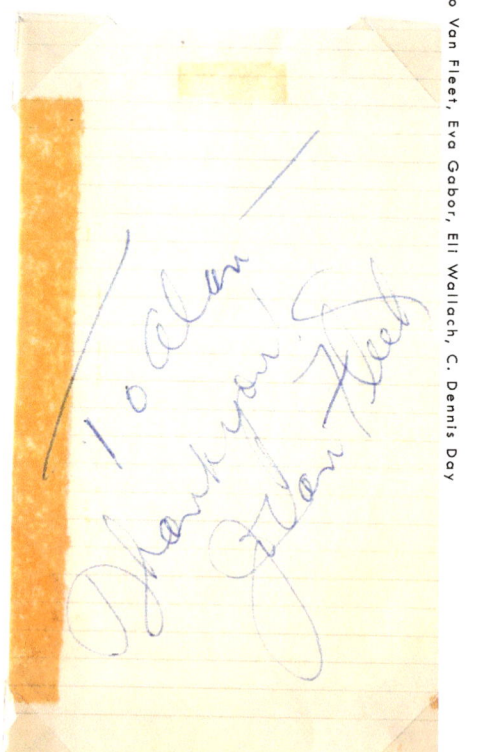

LTCW: Fred Clark, Anne Jackson, Cyril Ritchard, Jo Van Fleet, Eva Gabor, Eli Wallach, C. Dennis Day

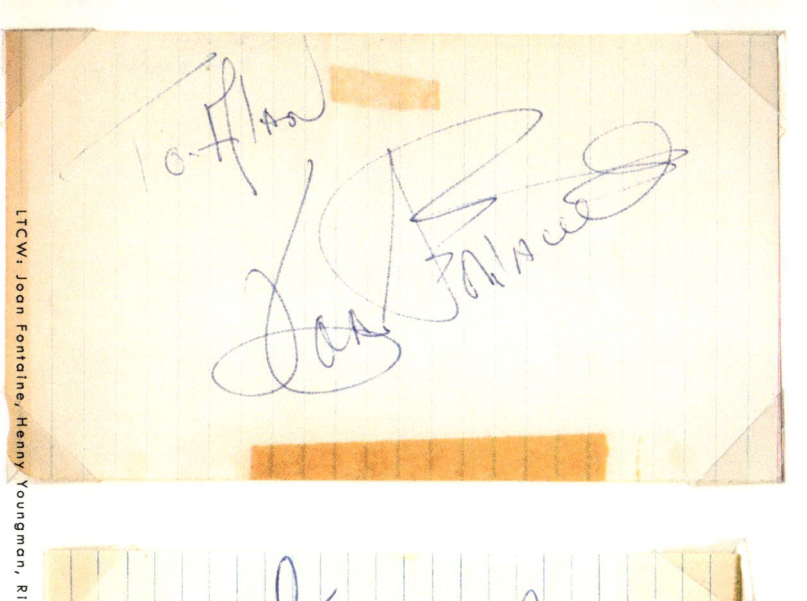
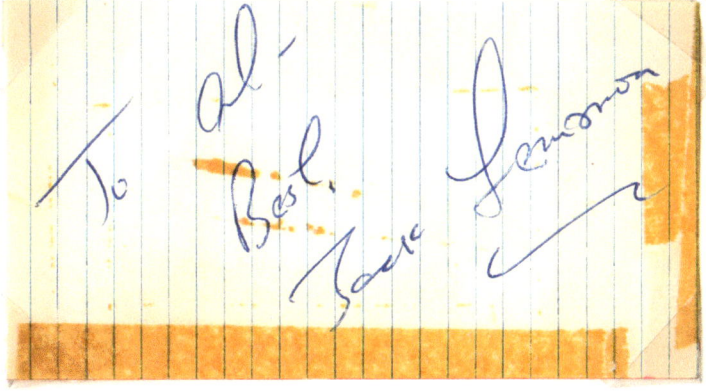

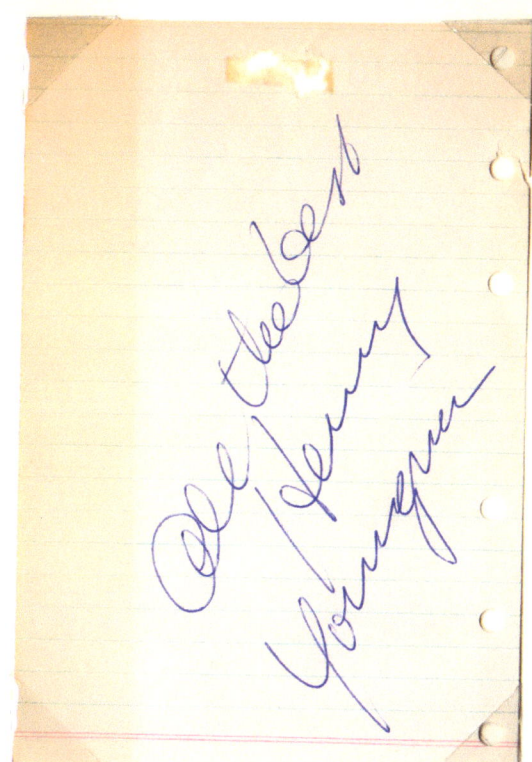
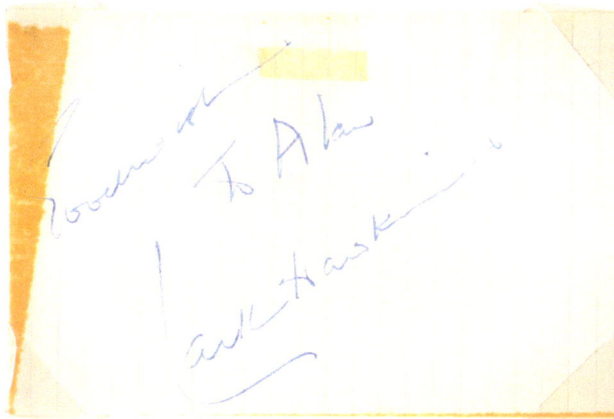
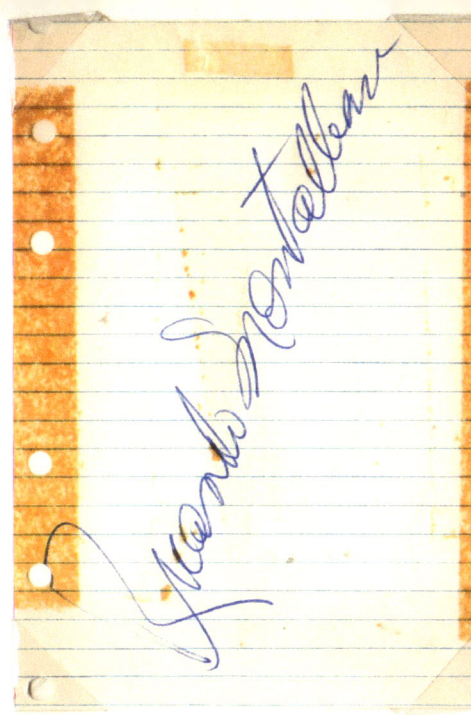

LTCW: Joan Fontaine, Henny Youngman, Ricardo Montalban, Anne Bancroft, Jack Hawkins, Sugar Ray Robinson, Jack Lemmon

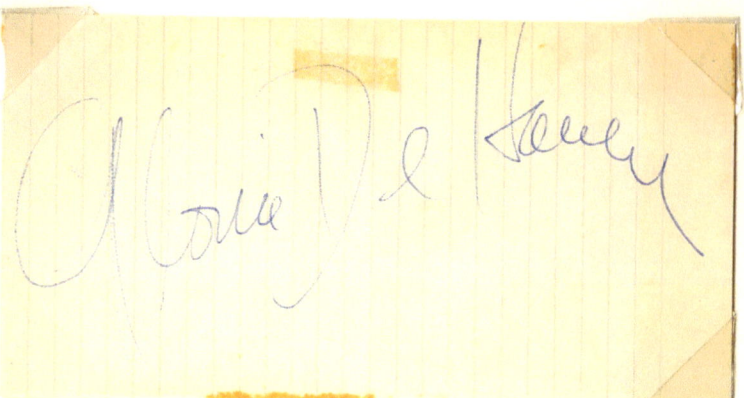
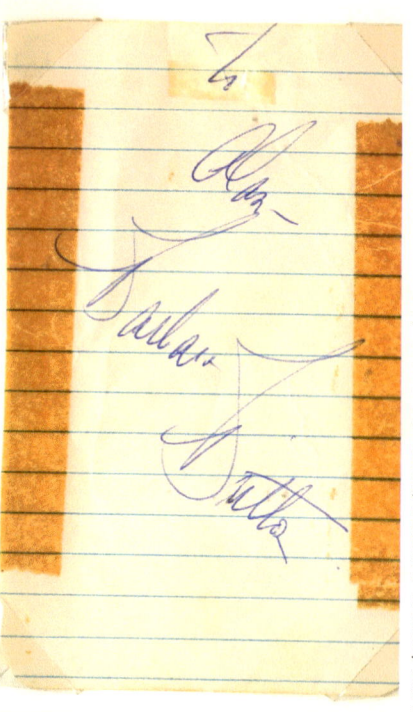

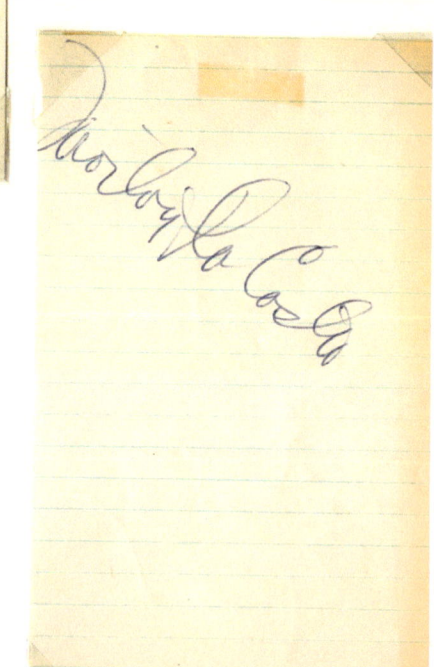

LTCW: Broderick Crawford, Gloria De Haven, Barbara Britton, Morton De Costa, June Haver, Bill Hayes, Ginger Rogers, C. Shelly Winters

LTCW; Judy Holliday, Sylvia Sidney, Martha Raye, Marlon Brando, Howard Keel, Sal Mineo, Doug Fairbanks

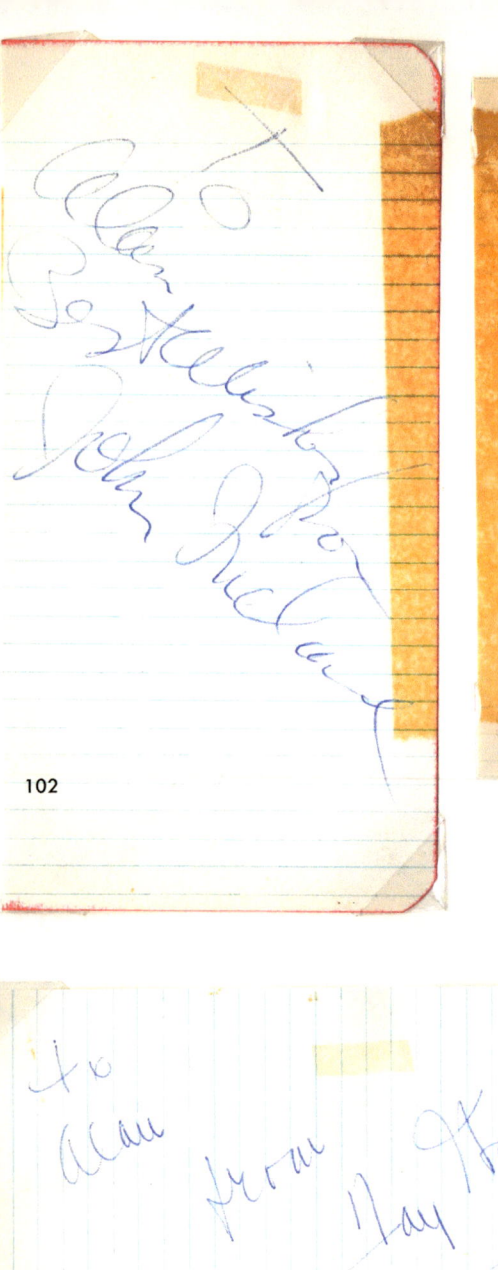
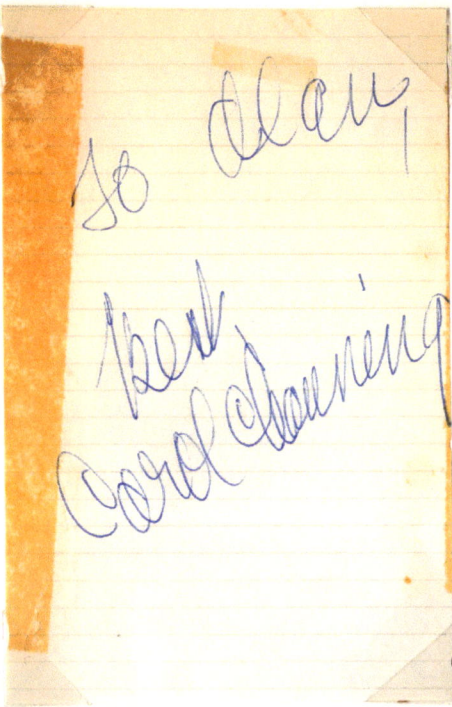
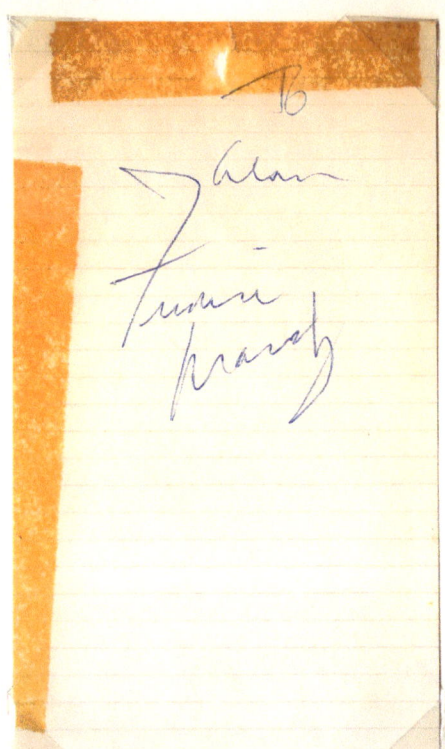
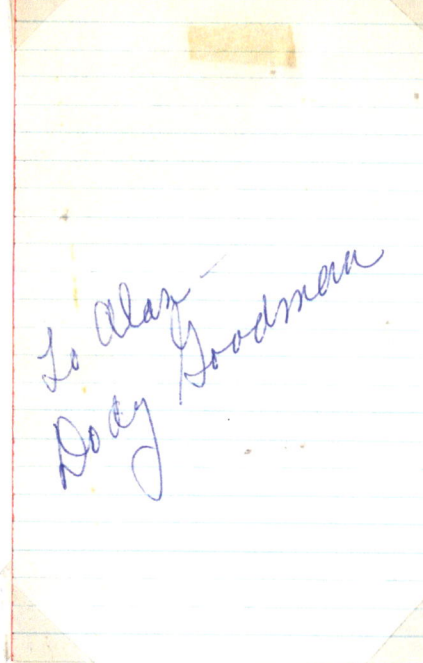

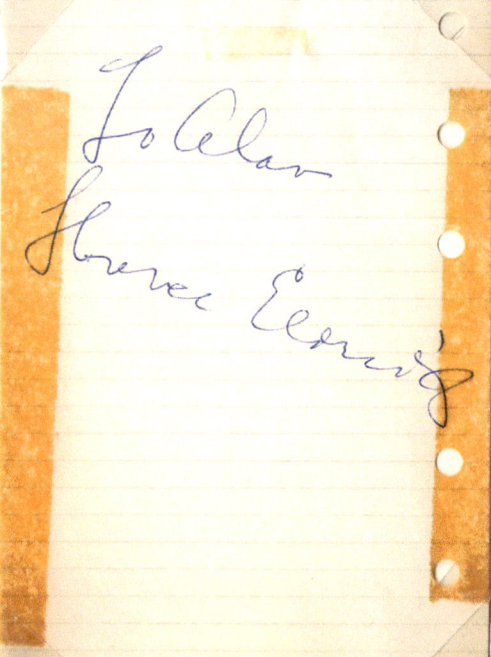

LTCW: John Ireland, Carol Channing, Frederick March, Dody Goodman, Mildred Natwick, Florence Eldridge, Fay Wray

LTCW: Maximillian Schell, Yul Brynner, David O. Selznick, Arthur Miller, Sid Lumet, Richard Basehart

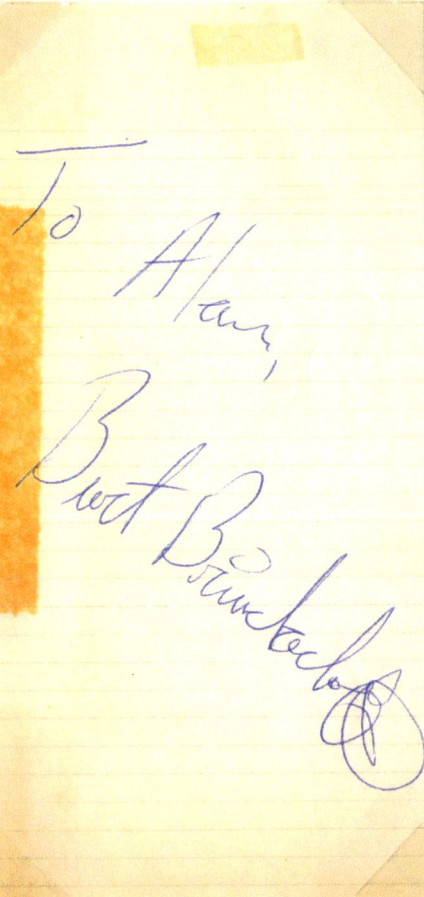
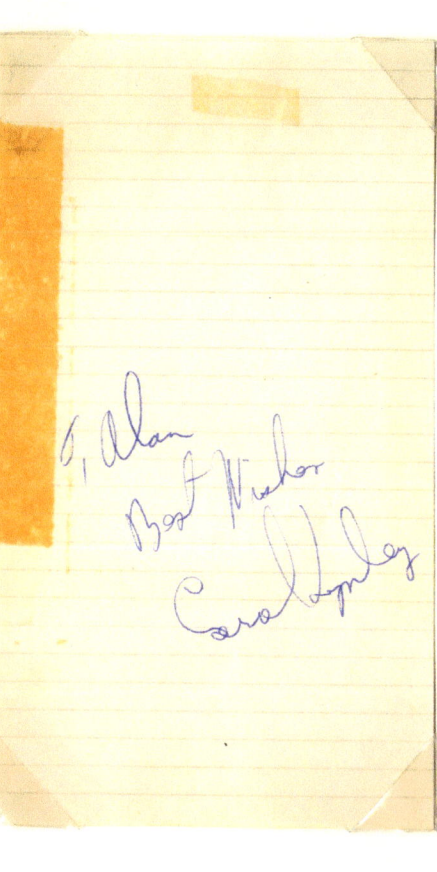
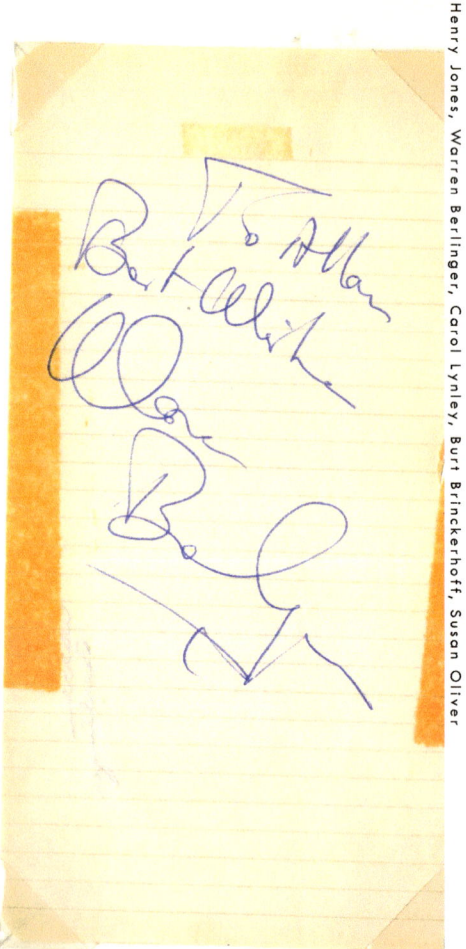

LTCW: Jackie Coogan, Henry Jones, Warren Berlinger, Carol Lynley, Burt Brinckerhoff, Susan Oliver

LTCW: Dennis Hopper, Chester Morris, Susan Strasberg, Viveca Lindfors, Shirley Booth, Don Murray, Janice Rule

105

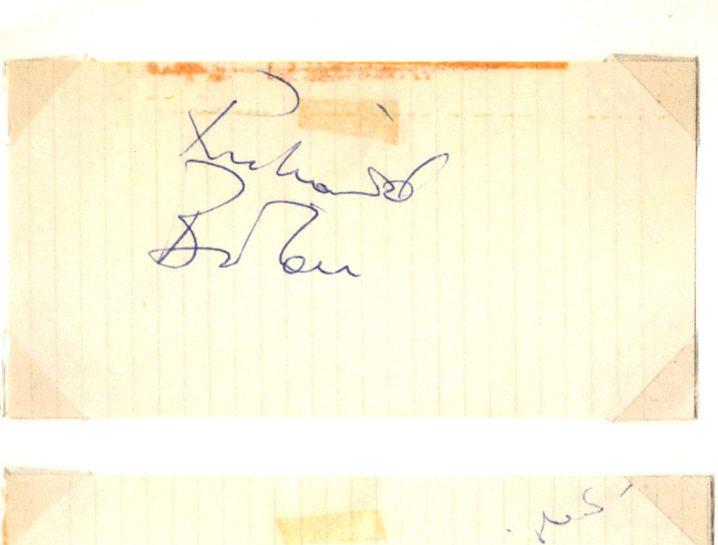
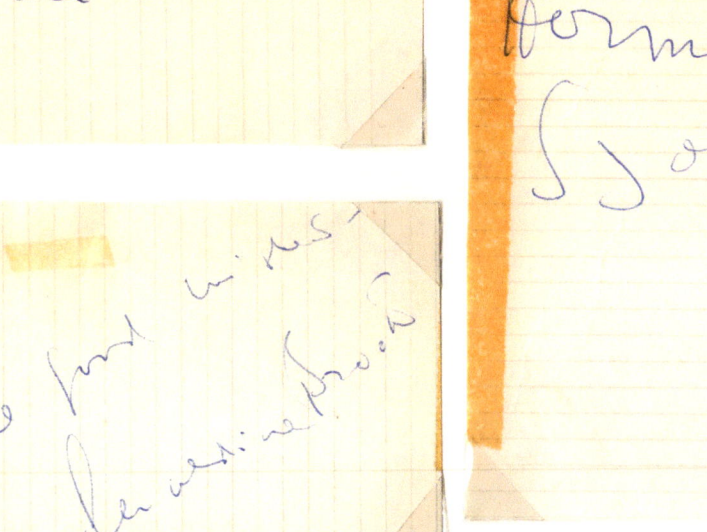
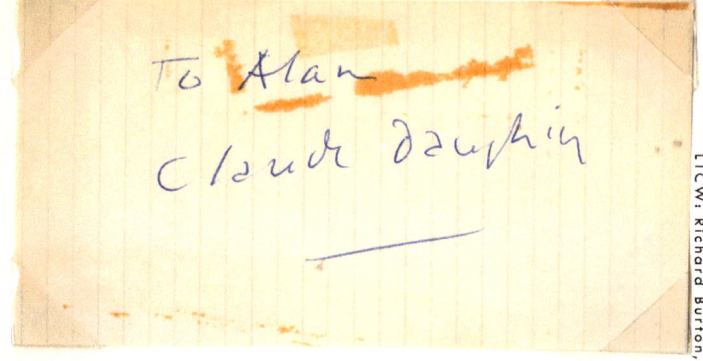
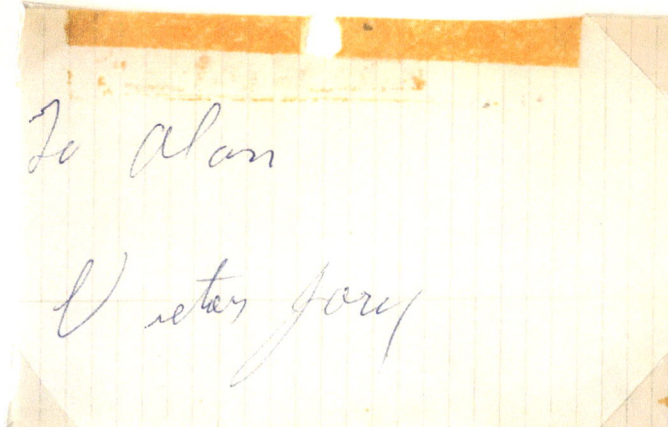
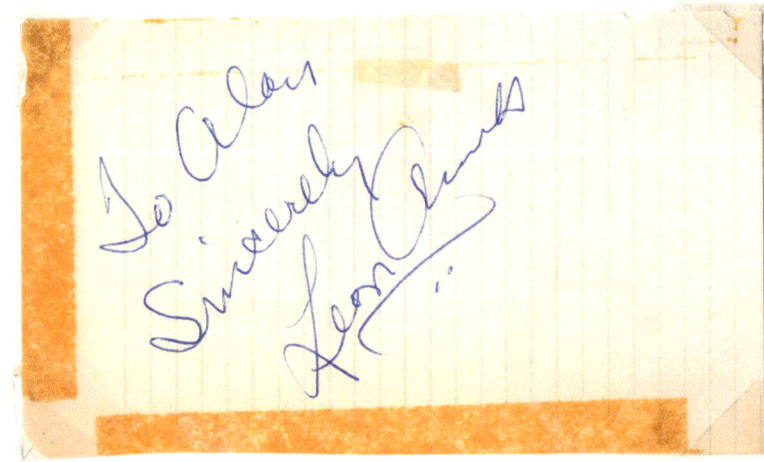
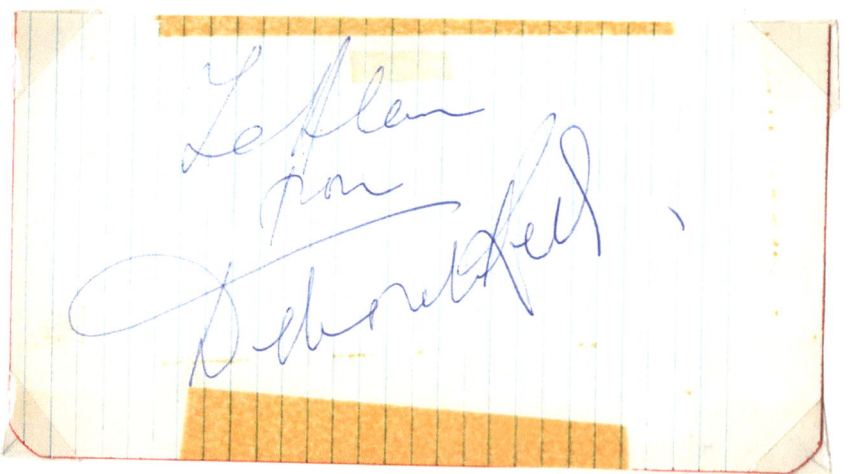

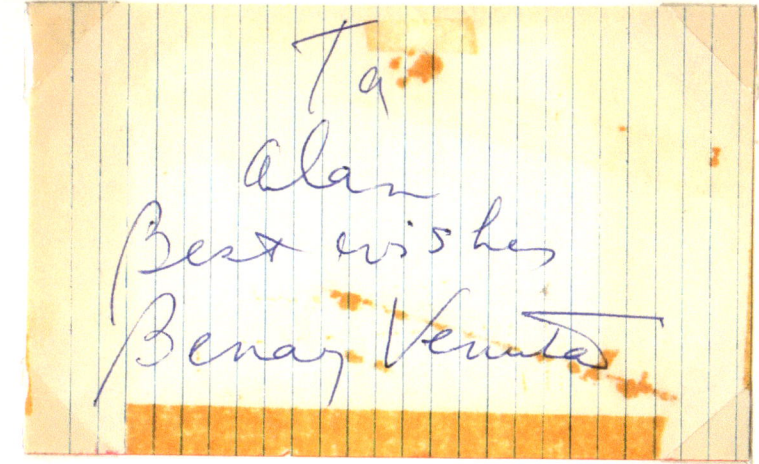

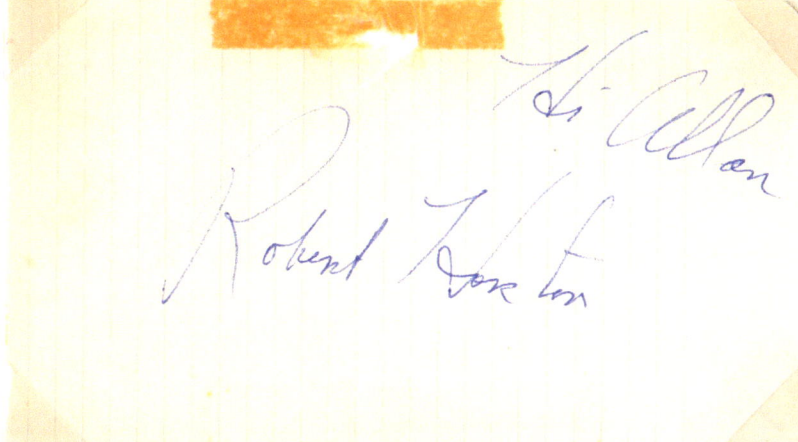

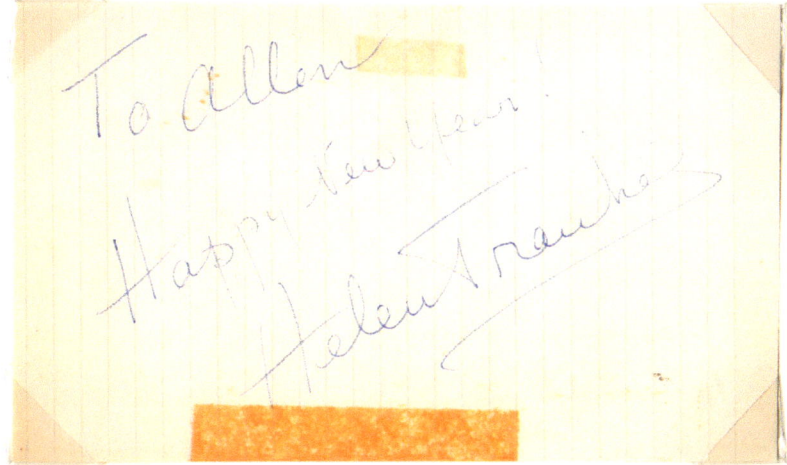

LTCW: Burgess Meredith, Benay Venuta, Mary Healy, Pat Boone, Helen Traubel, Robert Horton

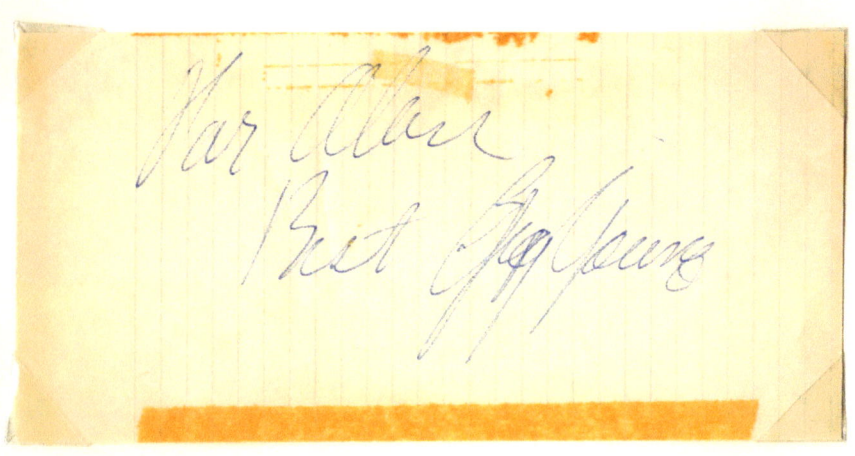
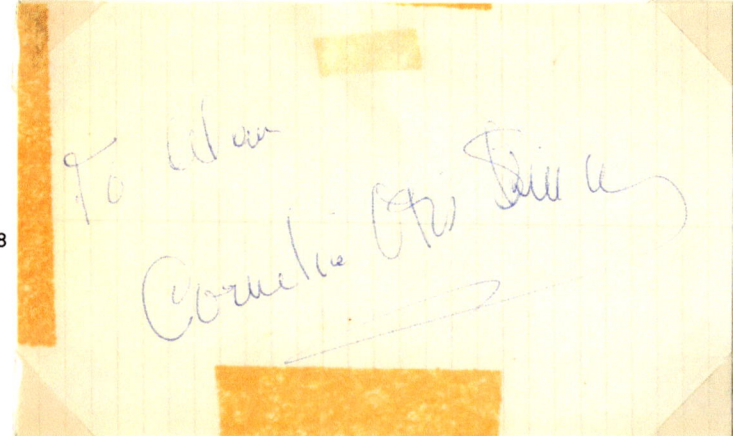

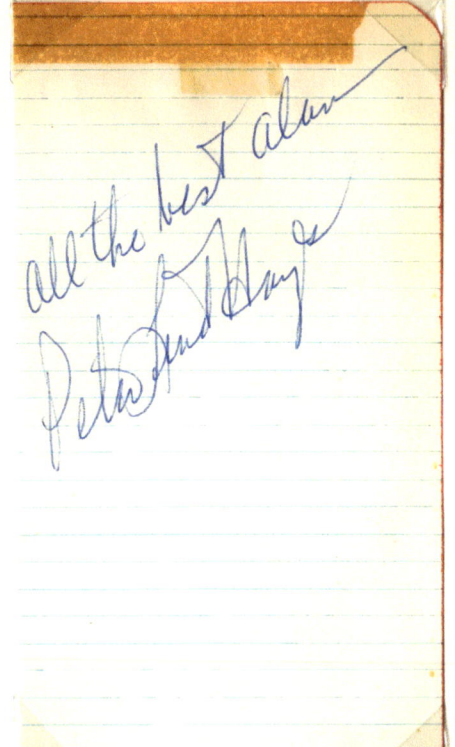
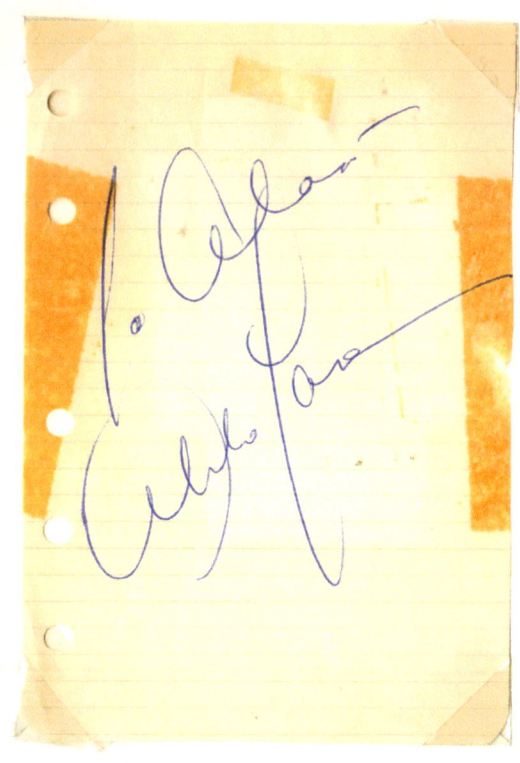
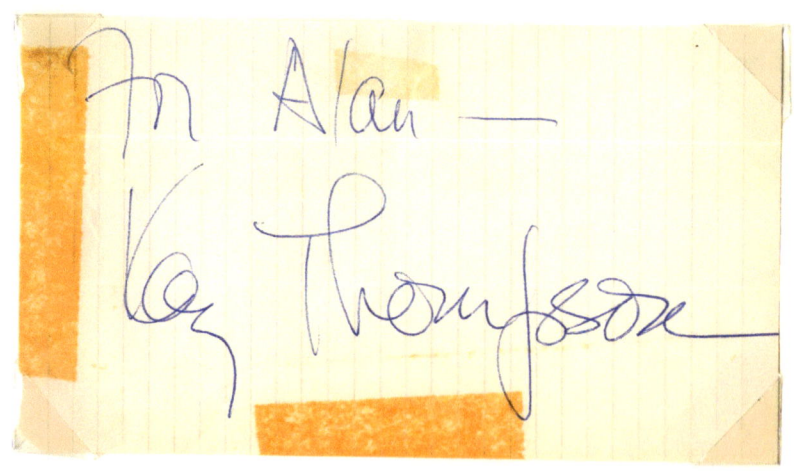

LTCW: Gig Young, Peter Lind Hayes, Abbe Lane, Kay Thompson, Dick Clark, Cornelia Otis Skinner

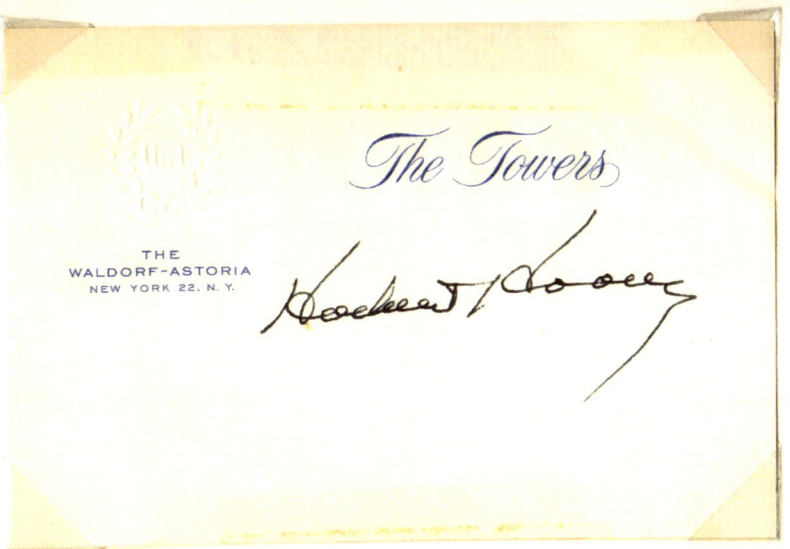
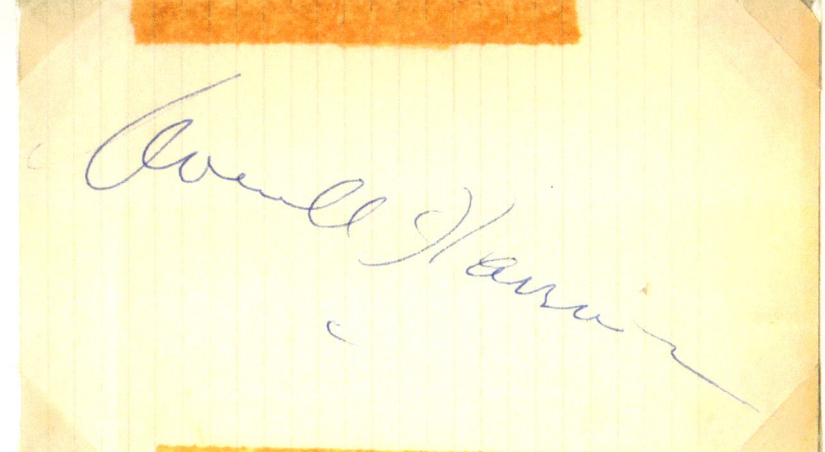
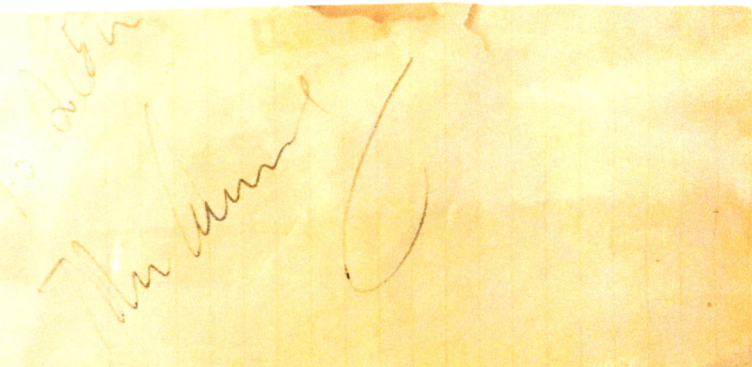

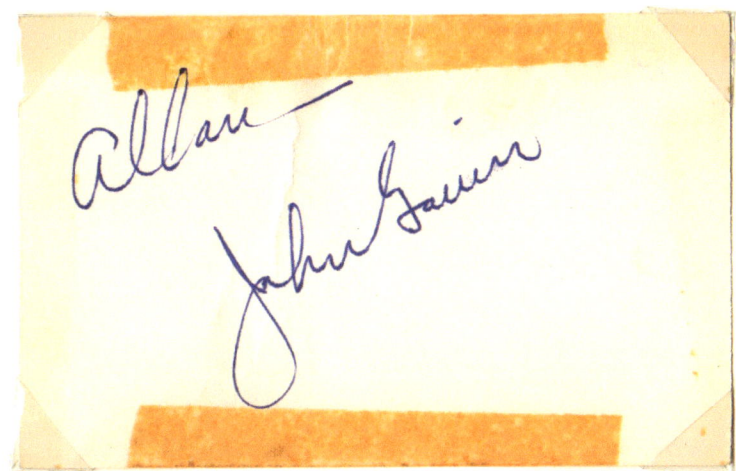

LTCW: Herbert Hoover, Averill Harriman, R. B. Meyner, John Gavin, Robert F. Wagner, John Kennedy

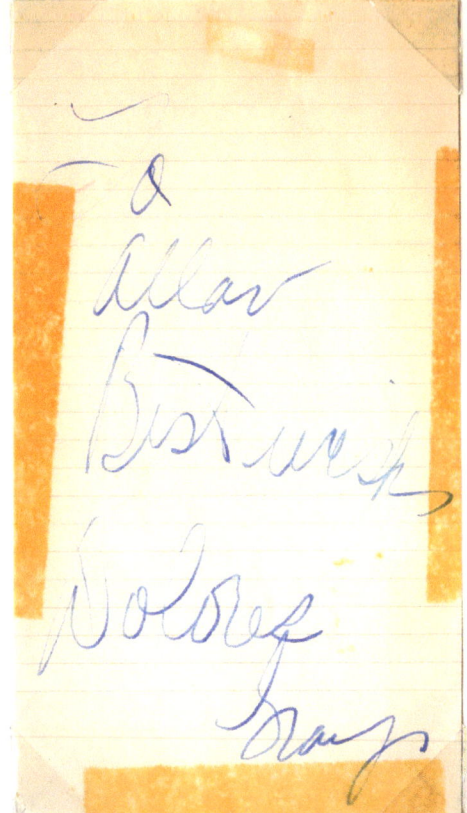
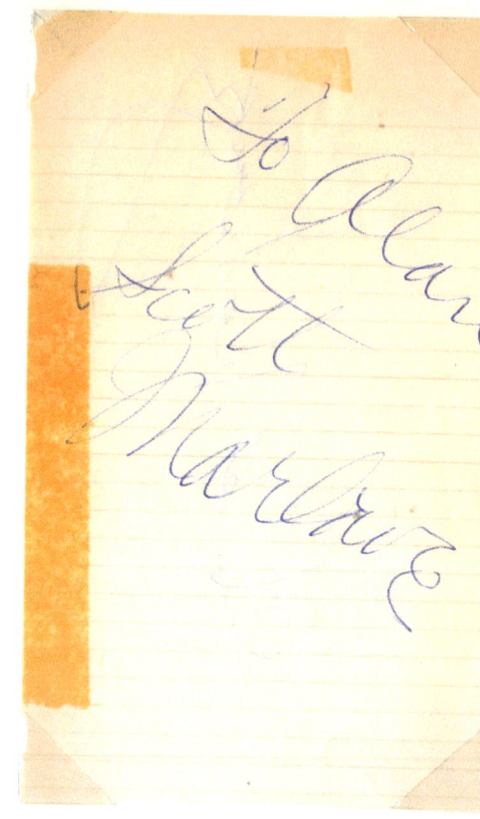
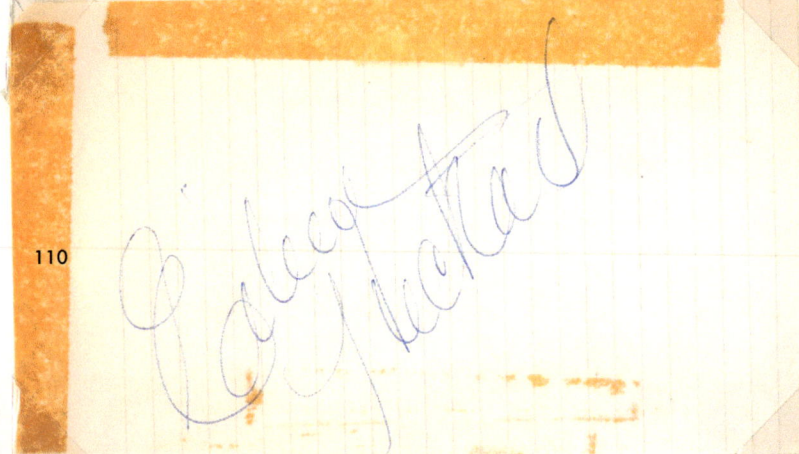
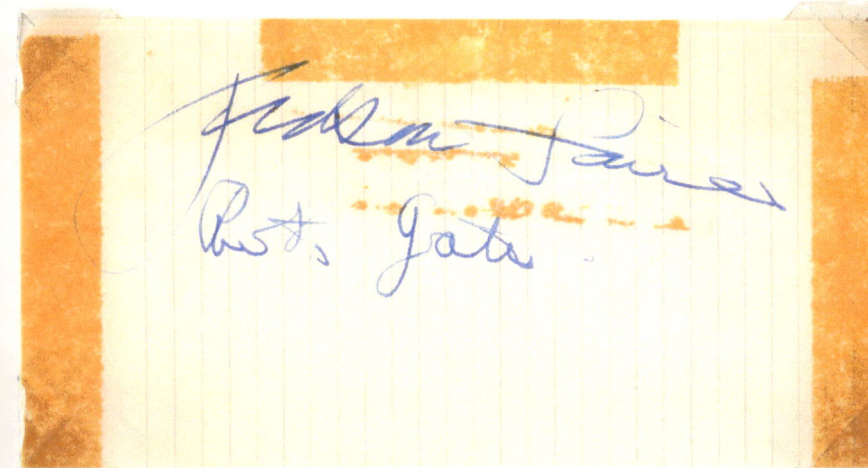

LTCW: Faye Emerson, Delores Gray, Scott Marlowe, Greer Garson, Judson Laire & Ruth Gates, Eileen Heckart

LTCW: Rod Steiger, Jimmy Stewart, Lisa Kirk, Toni Arden, Dan Duryea, Richard Egan, Johnny Johnston, C. Ray Bolger

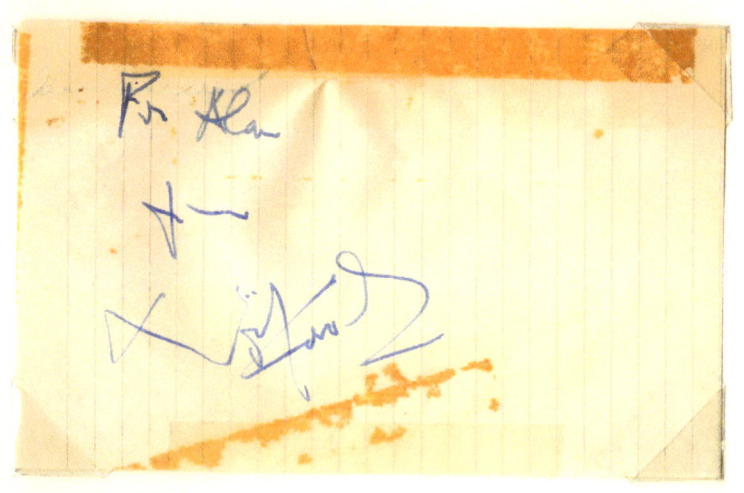
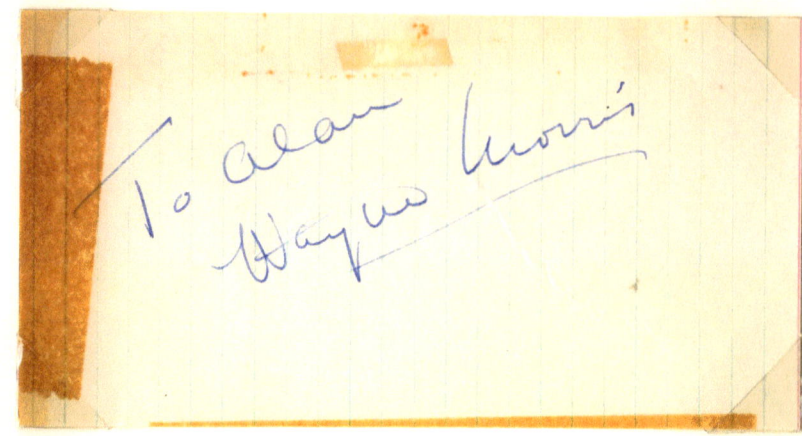
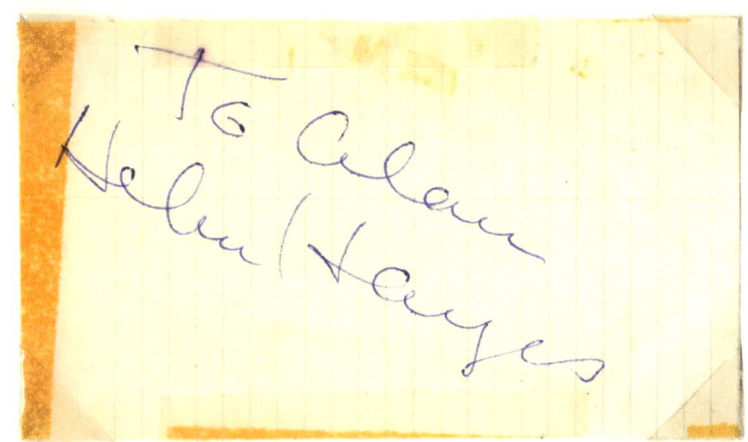
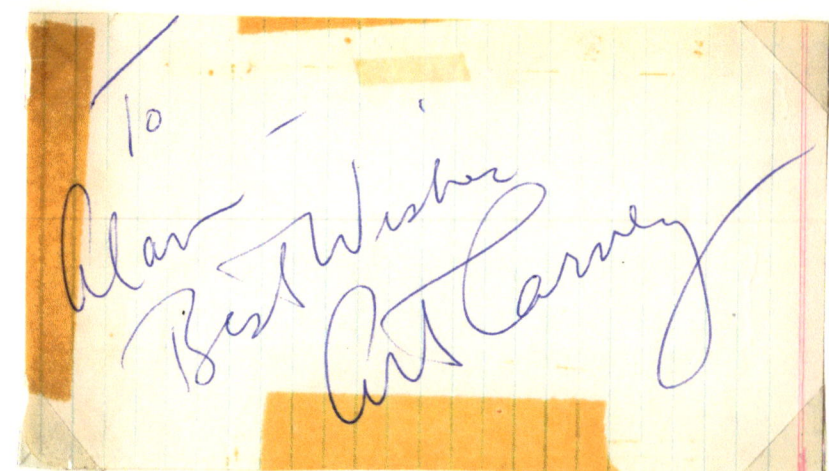
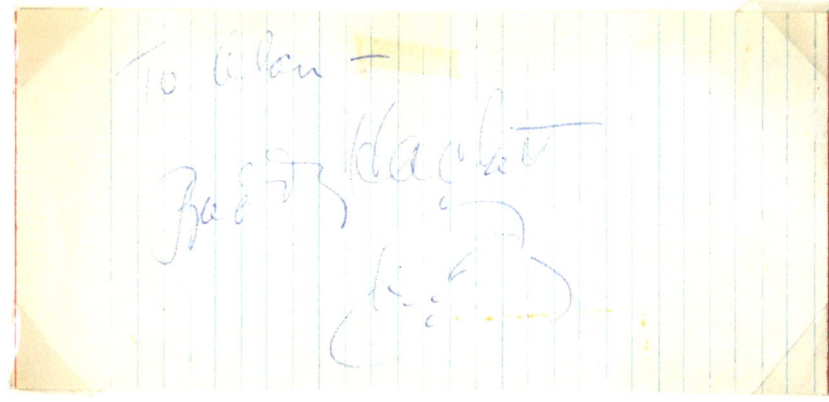
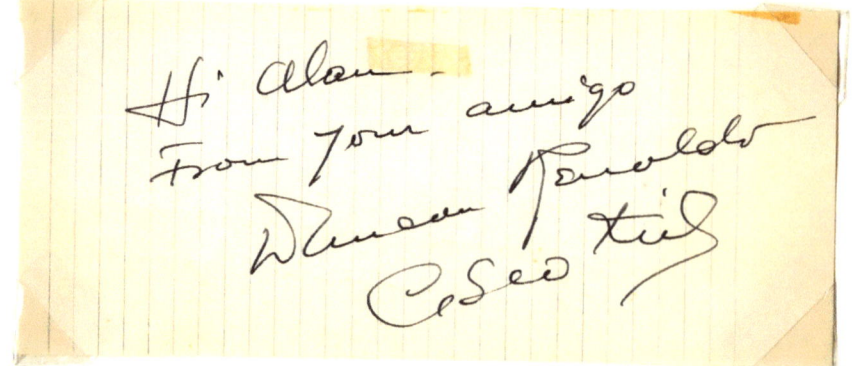

LTCW: Noel Coward, Wayne Morris, Art Carney, Duncan Rinaldo (Cisco Kid), Buddy Hackett, Helen Hayes

LTCW: Nat King Cole, Peggy Wood, Lee Remick, Jason Robards Jr., Teresa Wright, Rosalind Russell, Cedric Hardwick

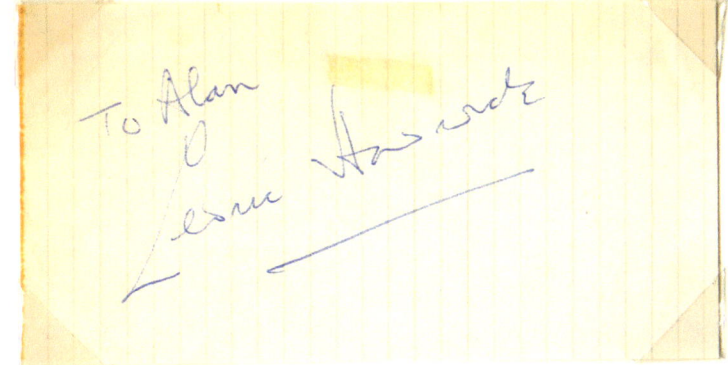

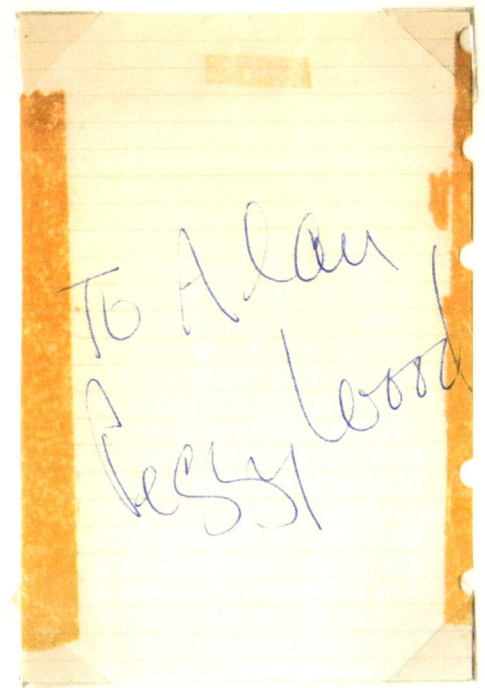
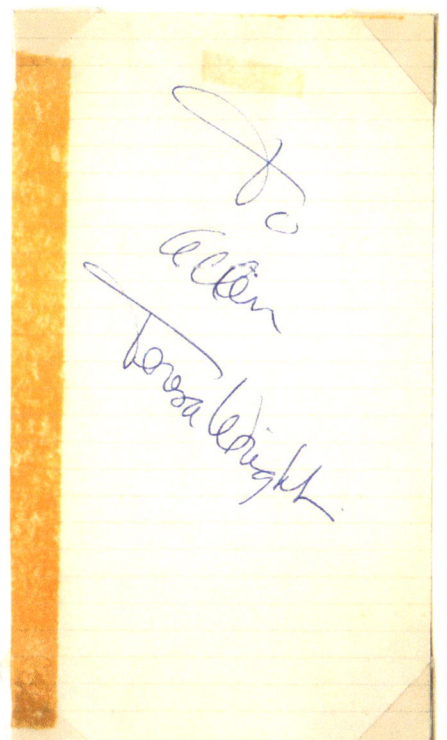
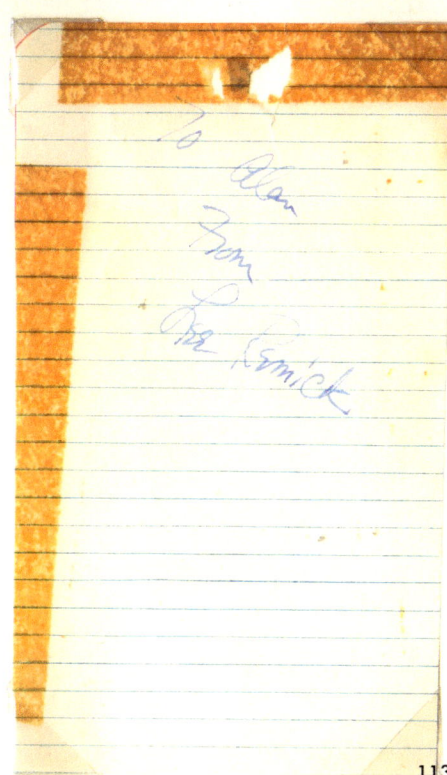
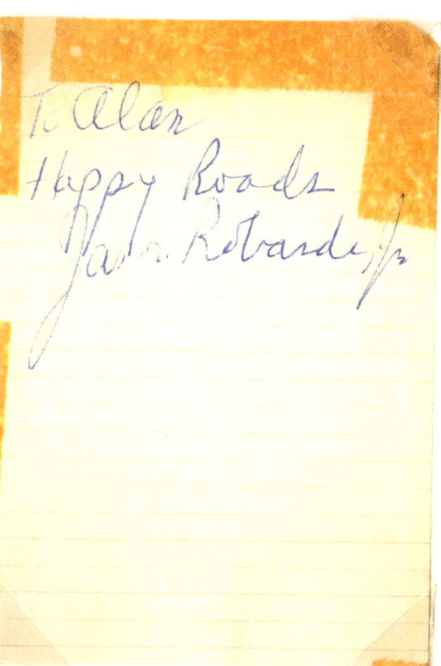

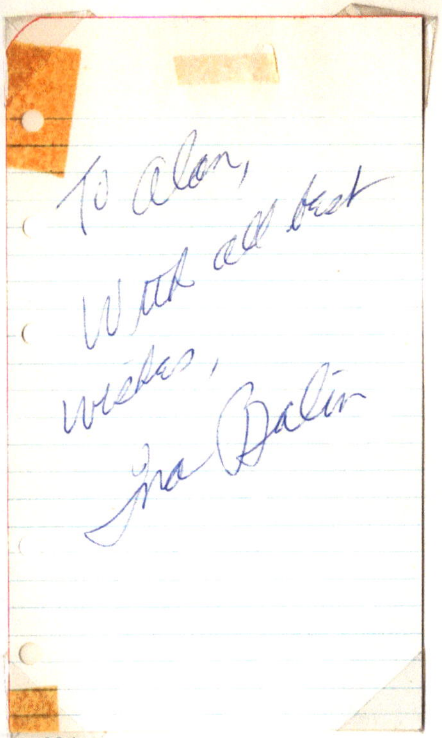

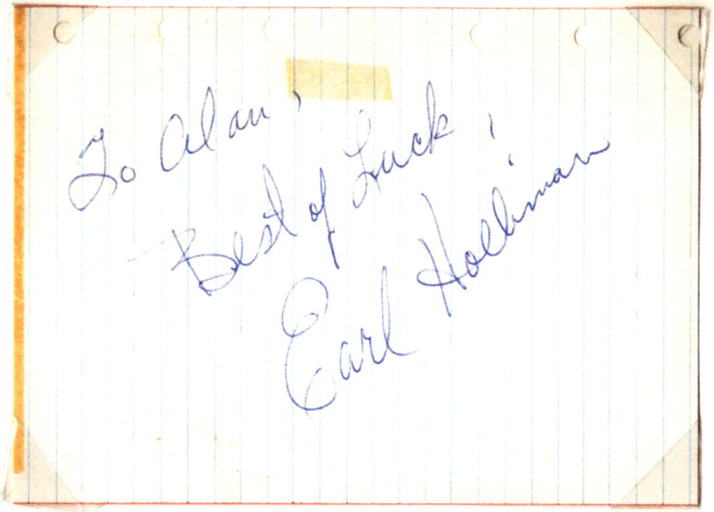

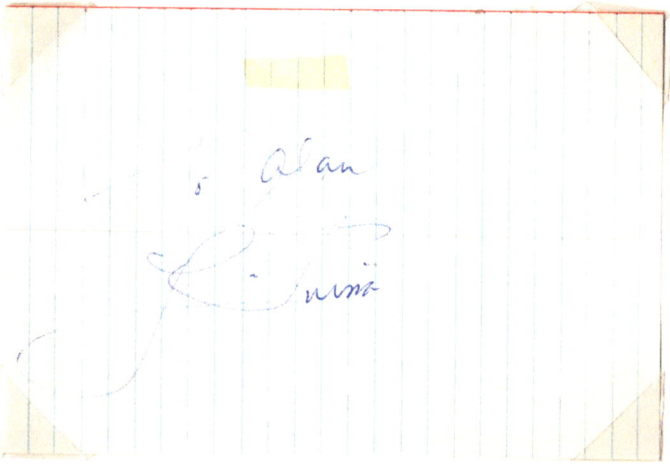

LTCW: Ina Balin, Earl Holliman, Keely Smith, Louis Prima, Ben Gazzara, Edward Andrews, Jack Carter

To Alan,
With all best wishes,
Ina Balin

To Alan,
Best of Luck!
Earl Holliman

Keely Smith

Edward Andrews

To Alan
Louis Prima

Jack Carter

To Alan
Ben Gazzara

LTCW: Roddy McDowell, Michael Constantine, Shirley MacLaine, Thelma Ritter, Agnes Moorehead, Mitch Miller, Julie Harris

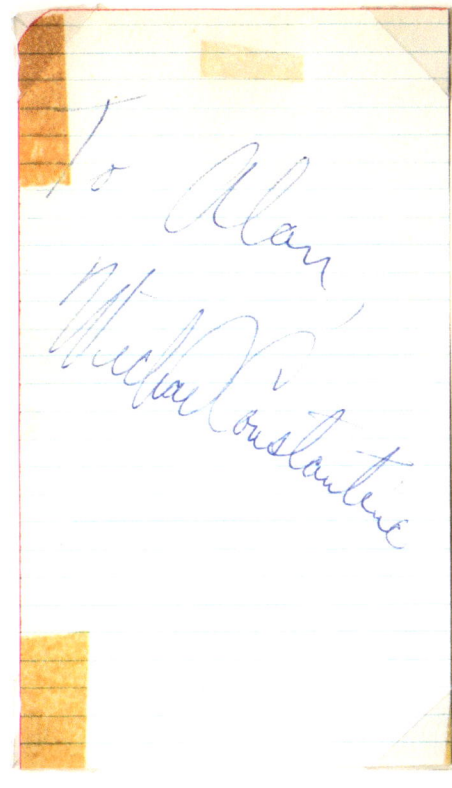
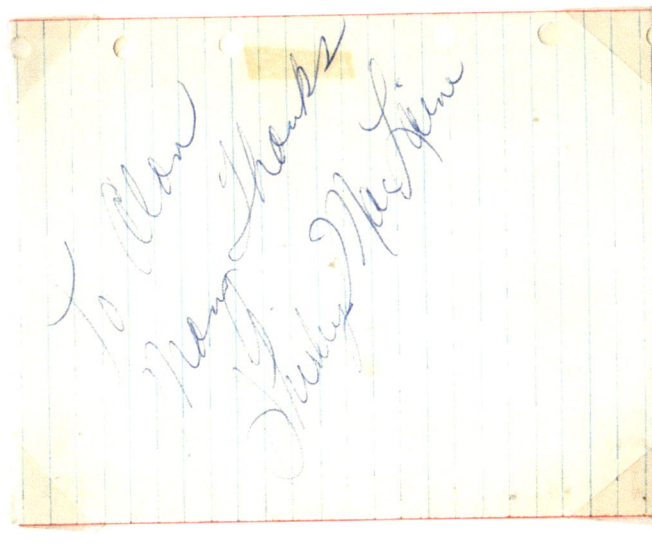

LTCW: Xavier Cugat, Giselle MacKenzie, Vaughn Monroe, Jack Benny, Thomas Mitchell, Peggy Ann Garner, Paul Ford, C. Dale Evans

LTCW: Sandra Dee, Don and Phil Everly, Jean Simmons, Gypsy Rose Lee, Snooky Lanson, Tony Bennett, Gena Rowlands, Andy Williams, C. Pearl Bailey

117

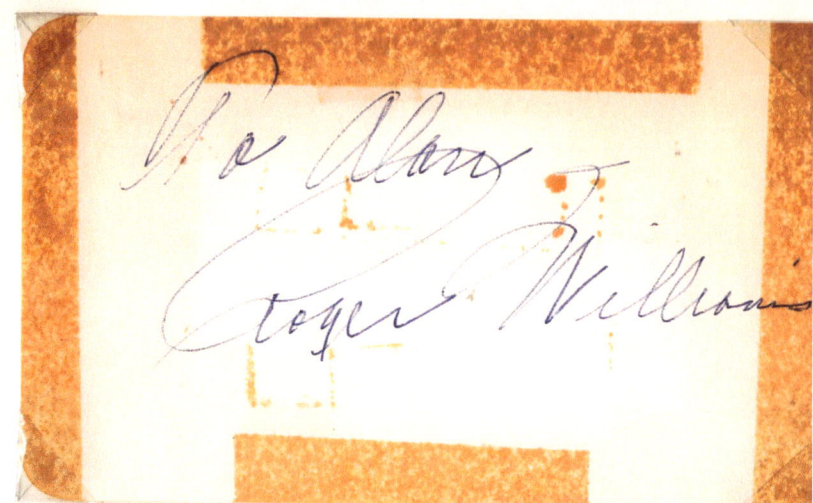
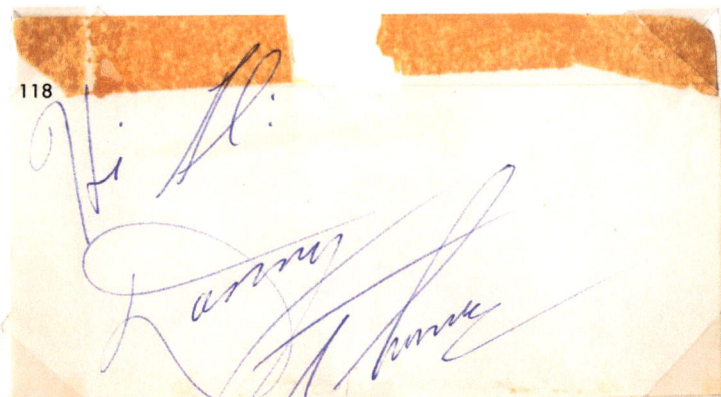
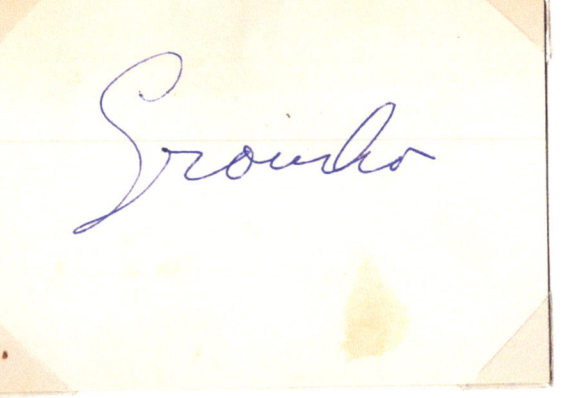
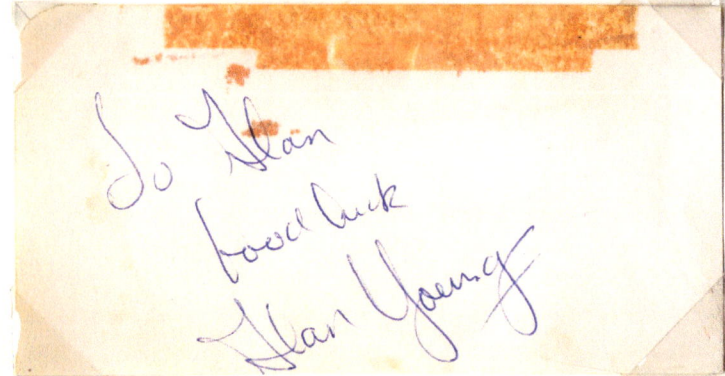
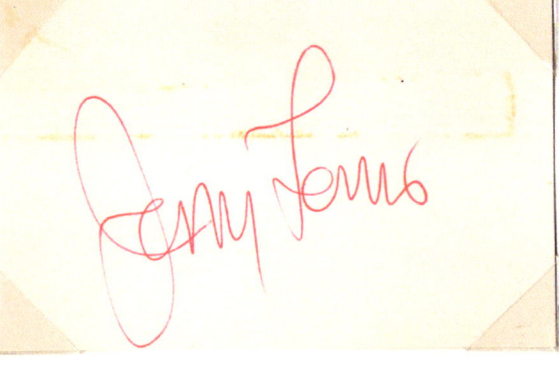

LTCW: George Nader, Darren McGavin, Roger Williams, Carol Burnett, Jerry Lewis, Alan Young, Danny Thomas, C. Groucho Marx

LTCW: Carol Haney, Alfred Drake, Alfred Hitchcock, Jackie Cooper, Joan Blondell, Phil Silvers, Kim Hunter, C. Lawrence Tierney

119

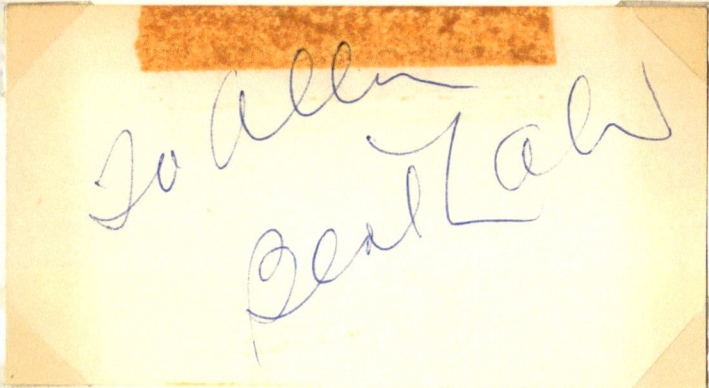

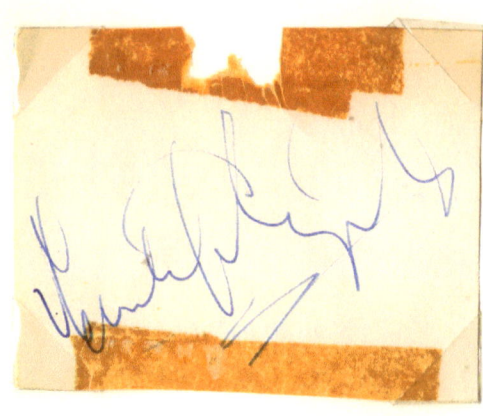
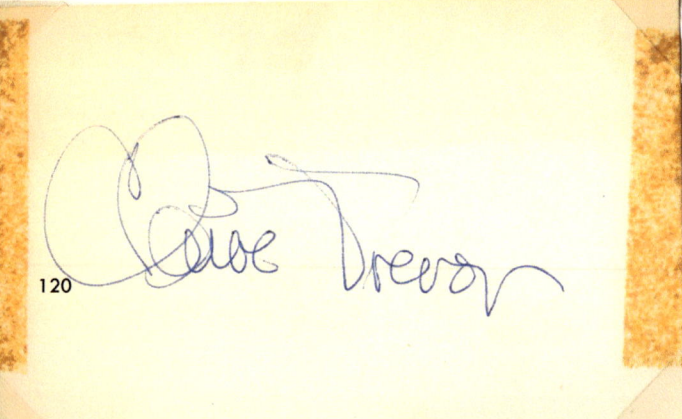

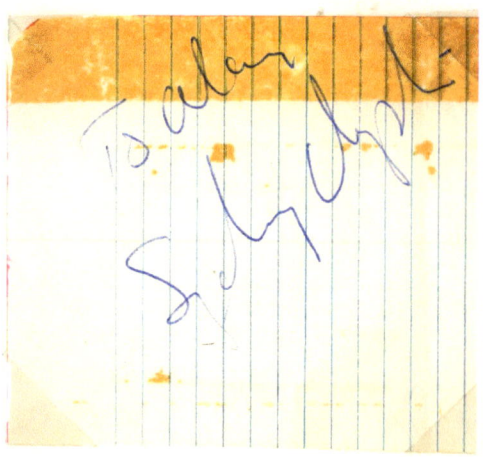
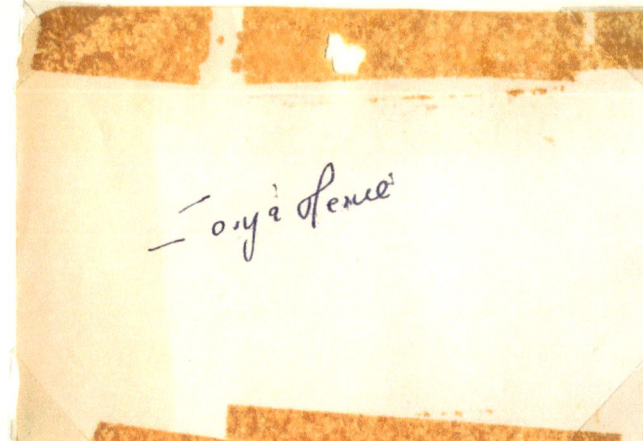
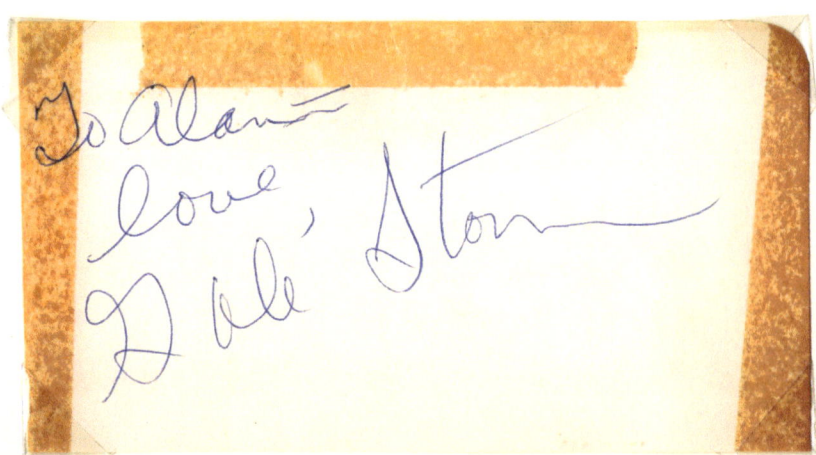

LTCW: Bert Lahr, Glenda Farrell, Carlton Carpenter, Sidney Chalpin, Gale Storm, Sonja Henie, Claire Trevor, C. Pete Palmer

LTCW: Walter Winchell, Don Taylor, Vera Ellen, Eva Marie Saint, Nita Talbo, Robert Preston

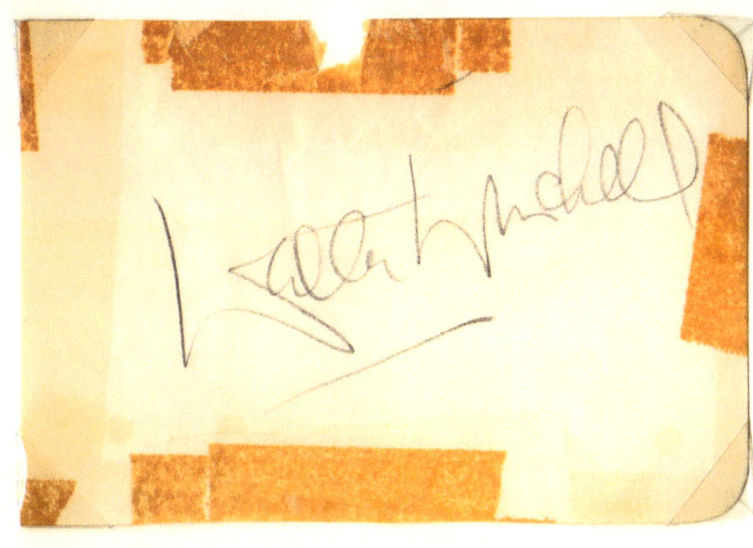

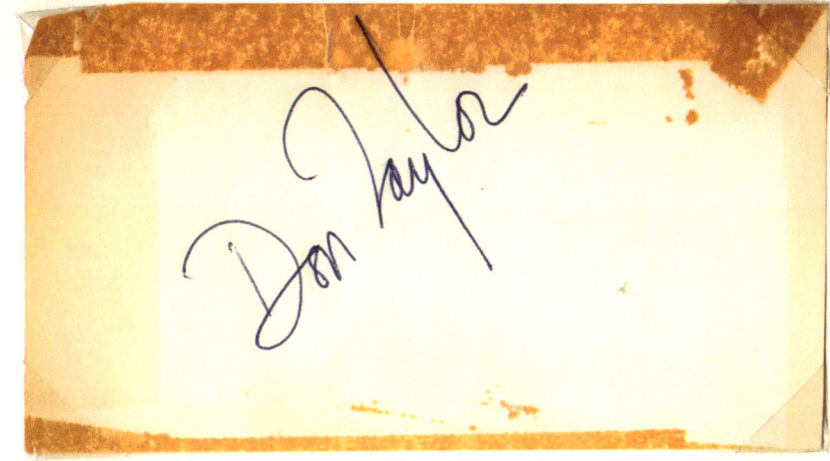
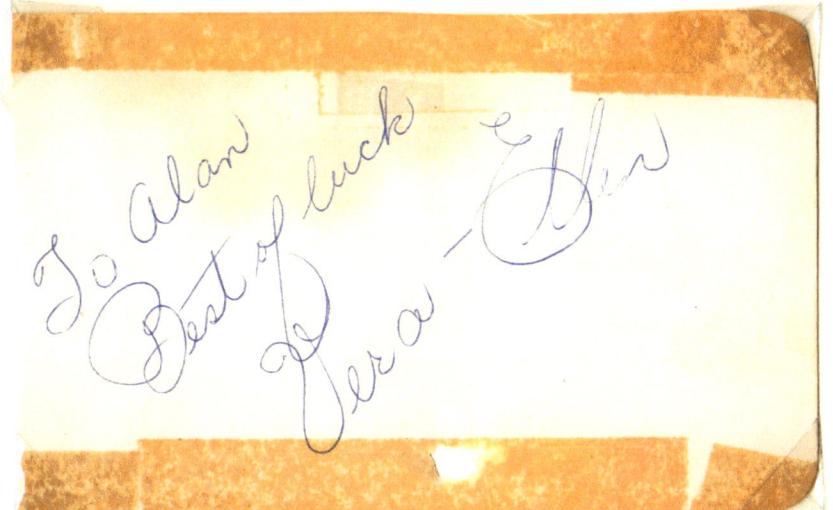
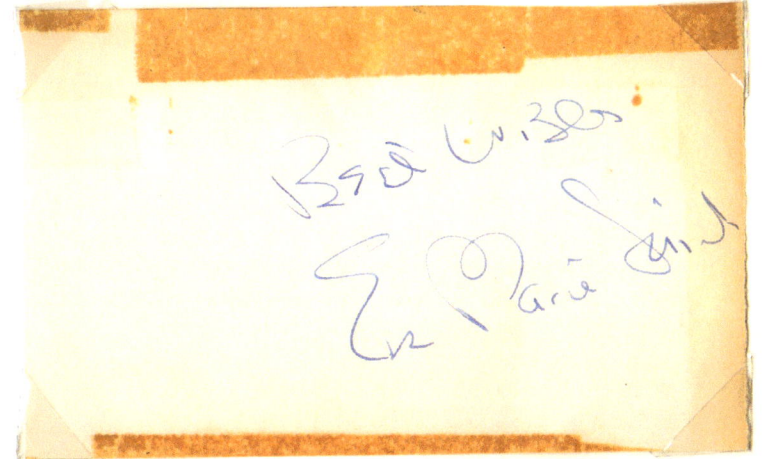

122

LTCW: Bess Myerson, Erin O'Brien, Donald Cook, Tony Curtis, Paul Douglas, Judy Tyler, C. James Dunn

LTCW: Steve Lawrence, Robert Young, Ed Wynn, Jim Garner, Jack Palance, Betsey Palmer, Mona Freeman, Edyie Gorme, C. Roberta Sherwood

123

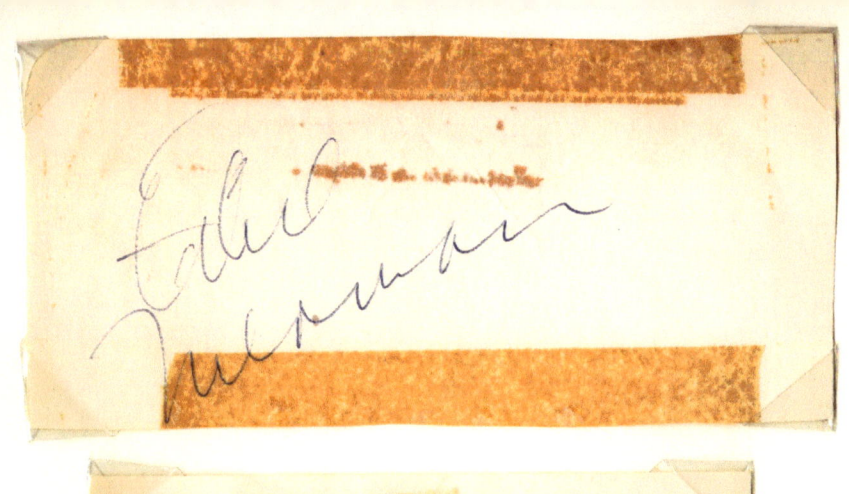
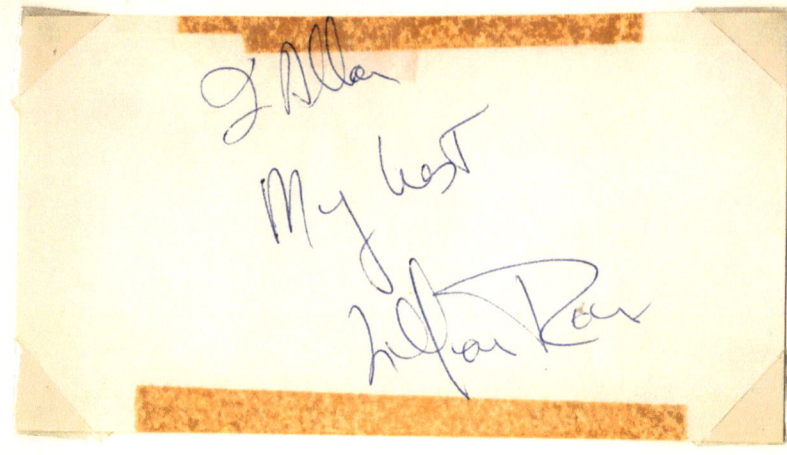
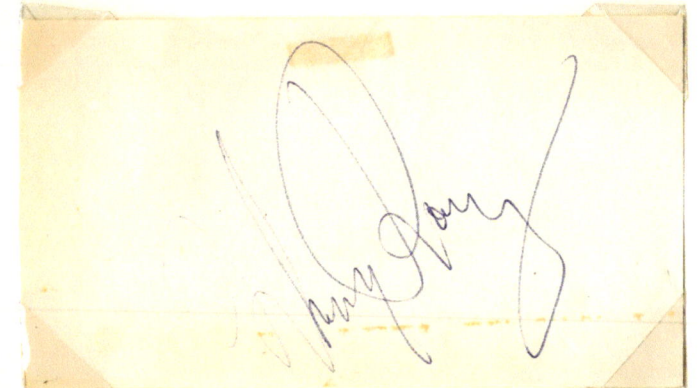
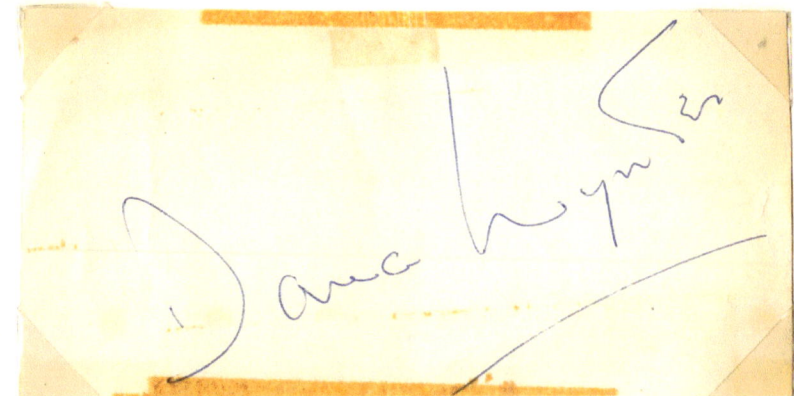
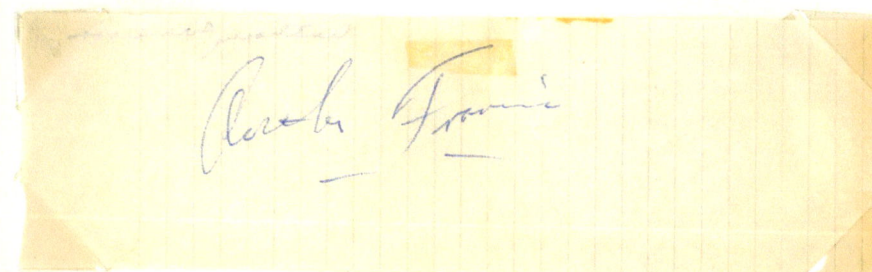

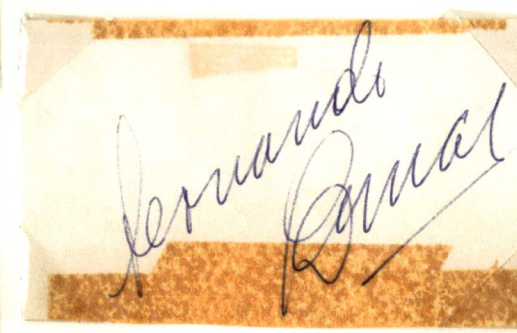

LTCW: Ethel Merman, Lillian Roth, Dana Wynter, Al Capp, Fernanado Lamos, Jim Arness, Anthony Franciosa, Johnny Ray

LTCW: Vic Damone, Anna Maria Alberghetti, Ed Sullivan, Tom Ewell, Penny Singleton, Julie London

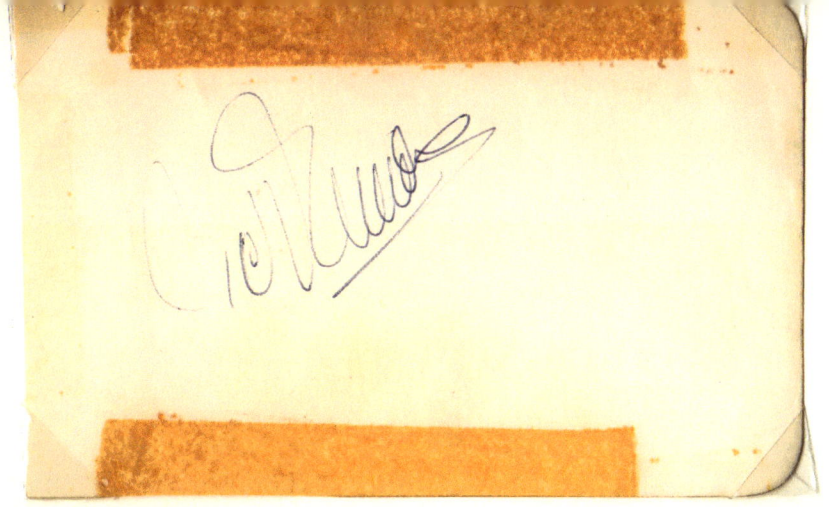
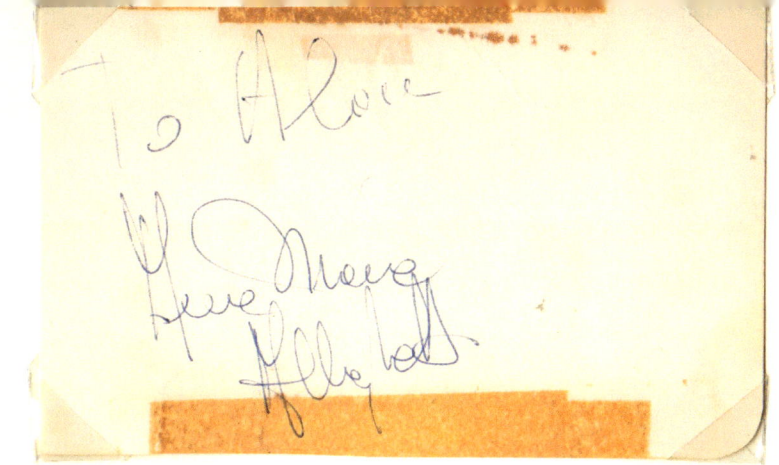
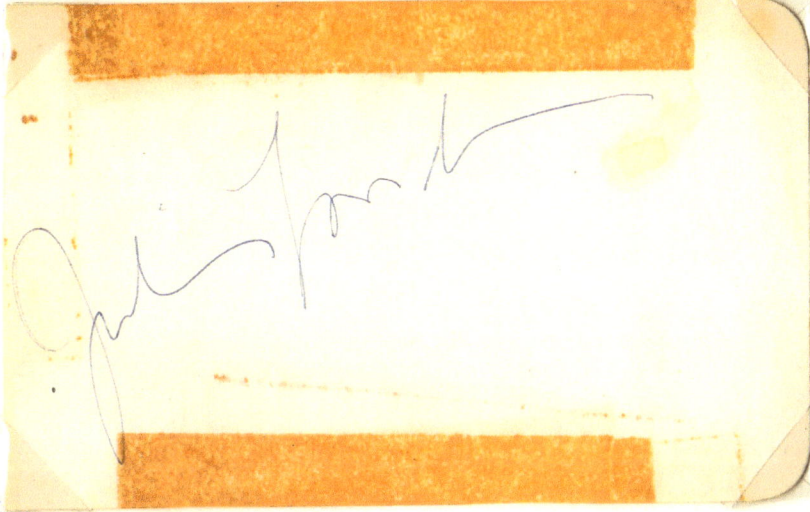
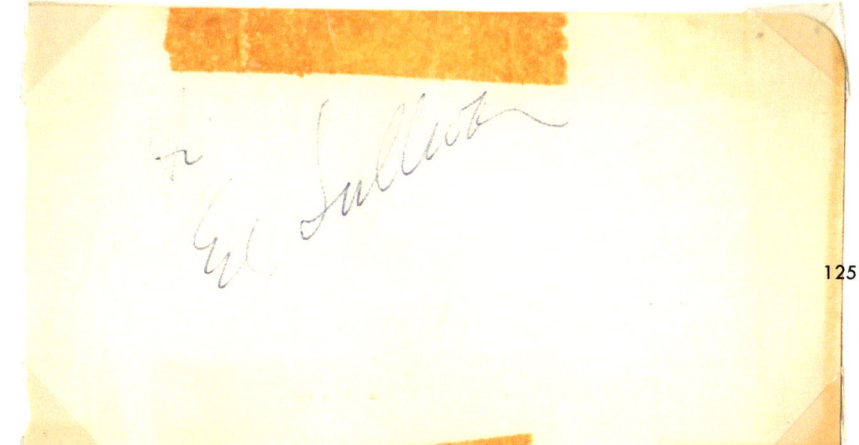
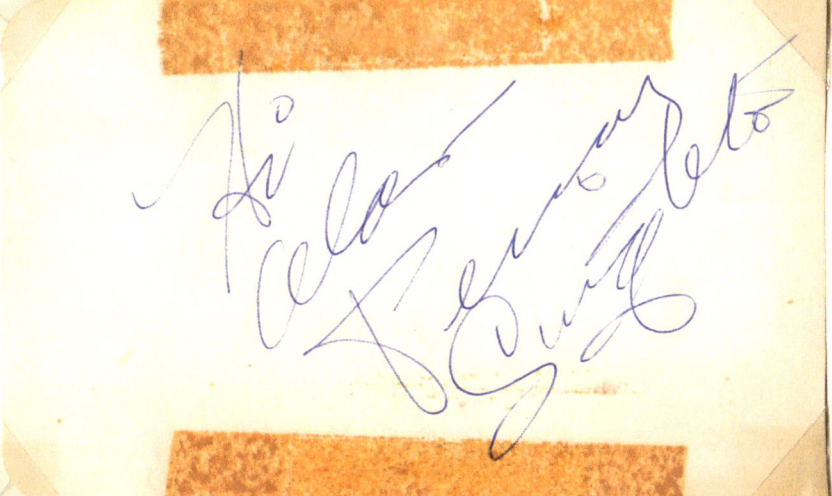

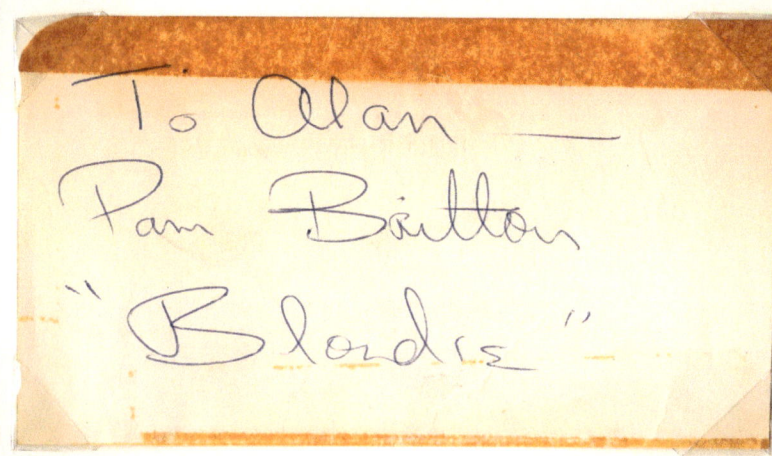
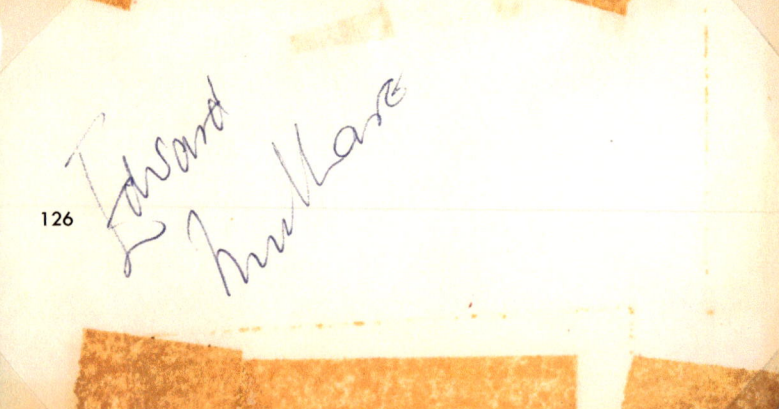

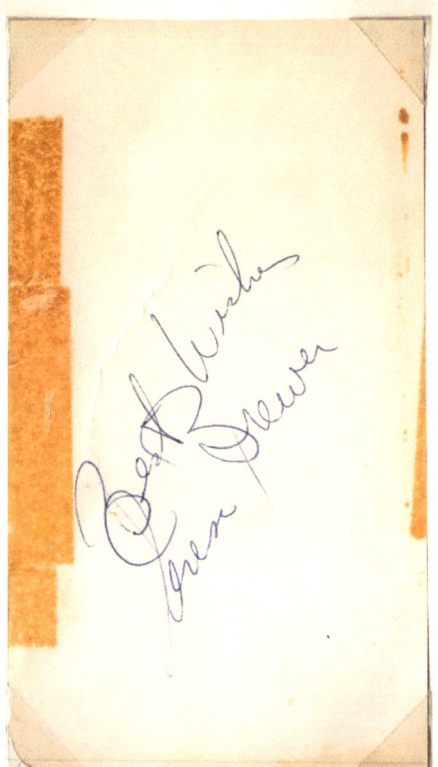

LTCW: Pamela "Blondie" Britton, Teresa Brewer, Walter Pidgeon, Julie Newmar, Jonathon Winters, Hope Emerson, Polly Bergen, Edward Mulhare, C. Gene Nelson

LTCW: Sarah Marshall, Gordon MacRae, Nancy Walker, Peter Ustinov, Eva Le Gallienne, Herbert Marshall, Andy Griffith, , Boots Mallory Marshall

From upper left: (cw) Martha Hyer, Don Murray, Eddie Hodges, Ann Blyth, Jean Pierre Aumont

Edie Adams Anna Maria Alberghetti Ben Alexander June Allyson Don Ameche Leon Ames Morey Amsterdam Judith Anderson Dana Andrews Edward Andrews Julie Andrews Eve Arden Toni Arden James Arness **Lauren Bacall** Pearl Bailey Carroll Baker Ina Balin Kaye Ballard Anne Bancroft Richard Basehart Count Basie Orson Bean Ralph Bellamy Tony Bennett Jack Benny Gertrude Berg Edgar Bergen Polly Bergen Milton Berle Warren Berlinger Theodore Bikel Vivian Blaine Joan Blondell Ray Bolger Pat Boone Shirley Booth Lee Bowman Jimmy Boyd Scott Brady Neville Brand Marlon Brando Teresa Brewer Burt Brinckerhoff Barbara Britton Pamela Britton John Bromfield Geraldine Brooks Yul Brynner Carol Burnett David Burns Richard Burton Red Buttons **Sid Caesar** James Cagney Al Capp Art Carney Carlton Carpenter John Carradine Pat Carroll Ken Carson Jack Carson Jack Carter John Cassavetes Carol Channing Sydney Chaplin Ilka Chase Maurice Chevalier Linda Christian Dane Clark Dick Clark Fred Clark Van Cliburn Claudette Colbert Nat King Cole Hans Conreid Michael Constantine Jackie Coogan Donald Cook Gary Cooper Jackie Cooper Katherine Cornell Jerome Cowan Noel Coward Richard Crenna Broderick Crawford Hume Cronyn Gary Crosby Xavier Cugat Tony Curtis **Morton DaCosta** Arlene Dahl Dan Dailey Lili Darvas Howard da Silva Claude Dauphin Ann B. Davis Sammy Davis Jr. Dennis Day Sandra Dee Gloria DeHaven Olivia De Havilland Albert Dekker Brandon DeWilde Diana Dors Kirk Douglas Paul Douglas Alfred Drake James Dunn Jimmy Durante Dan Duryea **Richard Egan** Anita Ekberg Florence Eldridge Vera Ellen Faye Emerson Hope Emerson Dale Evans Don and Phil Everly Timmy Everett Tom Ewell **Douglas Fairbanks** Glenda Farrell Mel Ferrer Betty Field Benny Fields Jo Van Fleet Henry Fonda Joan Fontaine The Fontane Sisters Scott Forbes Constance Ford Glenn Ford Paul Ford Tennessee Ernie Ford Anthony Franciosa Mona Freeman Jane Froman Betty Furness **Eva Gabor** Magda Gabor Eva Le Gallienne James Garner Peggy Ann Garner Greer Garson Ruth Gates John Gavin Mitzi Gaynor Ben Gazzara Peter Gennaro Alice Ghostley Georgia Gibbs Hermione Gingold Paulette Goddard Dody Goodman Gale Gordon Edyie Gorme Kathryn Grant Dolores Gray Adolph Green Joyce Grenfell Andy Griffith **Buddy Hackett** Carol Haney Cedric Hardwick Averill Harriman Julie Harris Rex Harrison Jack Hawkins June Haver Bill Hayes Peter Lind Hayes Helen Hayes Mary Healy Ben Hecht Eileen Heckart Van Heflin Sonja Henie Alfred Hitchcock Eddie Hodges Judy Holiday Earl Holliman Celeste Holm Herbert Hoover Bob Hope Dennis Hopper Hedda Hopper Geoffrey Horne Lena Horne Robert Horton Sally Ann Howes Marsha Hunt Kim Hunter Tab Hunter Will Hutchins Martha Hyer **John Ireland Anne Jackson** Zizi Jeanmaire George Jessel Johnny Johnston Henry Jones Victor Jory **Kurt Kasner**

The Autographs

Elia Kazan Howard Keel Emmitt Kelly Gene Kelly Kay Kendall John F. Kennedy Deborah Kerr John Kerr Richard Kiley Clint Kimbrough Lisa Kirk Phyllis Kirk Don Knotts Susan Kohner **Bert Lahr** Fernando Lamas Judson Laire Abbe Lane Hope Lange Snooky Lanson Piper Laurie Carol Lawrence Steve Lawrence Gypsy Rose Lee Janet Leigh Margret Leighton Jack Lemmon Sam Levine Jerry Lewis Joe E. Lewis Liberace Viveca Lindfors Frederick Loewe Gina Lollobrigida Julie London Denise Lor Sidney Lumet Carol Lynley **Giselle MacKenzie** Fred MacMurray Gordon MacRae James MacArthur Shirley MacLaine Karl Malden Marcel Marceau Frederic March Scott Marlowe Boots Mallory Herbert Marshall Sara Marshall Dick Martin Groucho Marx Kevin McCarthy Joan McCracken Patty McCormack Roddy McDowell Darren McGavin Dorothy McGuire Phyllis McGuire Horace McMahon Jayne Meadows Ralph Meeker Burgess Meredith Ethel Merman Scott Merrill Robert B. Meyner Arthur Miller Mitch Miller Sal Mineo Thomas Mitchell Vaughn Monroe Ricardo Montalban Terry Moore Agnes Moorehead Rita Moreno Jaye P. Morgan Robin Morgan Chester Morris Wayne Morris Edward Mulhare Don Murray Bess Myerson **George Nader** Mildrid Natwick Anna Neagle Patricia Neal Gene Nelson Cathleen Nesbit Paul Newman Julie Newmar David Niven **Hugh O'Brian** Erin O'Brien Maureen O'Hara Dennis O'Keefe Susan Oliver Laurence Olivier **Jack Paar** Jack Palance Betsy Palmer Peter Palmer Fess Parker Larry Parks Patachou Alice Pearce George Peppard Tony Perkins Jane Pickens Walter Pidgeon Sidney Poitier Jane Powell Tyrone Power Robert Preston Louis Prima Cameron Prudhomme **Anthony Quayle** **John Raitt** Vera Ralston Tony Randall Johnnie Ray Martha Raye Gene Raymond Donna Reed Carl Reiner Lee Remick Duncan Renaldo Cyril Ritchard Thelma Ritter Jason Robards Cliff Robertson Sugar Ray Robinson Ginger Rogers Ruth Roman Cesar Romero Barney Ross Lillian Roth Gena Rowlands Evelyn Rudie Janice Rule Rosalind Russell **Eva Marie Saint** George Sanders Tommy Sands Dore Schary Martha Scott Blossom Seeley David O. Selznick William Shatner Roberta Sherwood Sylvia Sydney Phil Silvers Jean Simmons Penny Singleton Cornelia Otis Skinner Keely Smith Howard St. John Rod Steiger Jan Sterling Jimmy Stewart Gale Storm Dean Stockwell Lee Strasberg Susan Strasberg Ed Sullivan Gloria Swanson **Phyllis Thaxter** Mel Torme Rip Torn Shirley Temple Helen Traubel Kay Thompson Danny Thomas Lawrence Tierney Claire Trevor Nita Talbot Don Taylor Judy Tyler Forrest Tucker **Peter Ustinov** **Gloria Vanderbilt** Benay Venuta Gwen Verdon **Bob Wagner** Robert F. Wagner Nancy Walker Eli Wallach Ethel Waters David Wayne Orson Wells Brooks West James Whitmore Kathleen Widdows Andy Williams Esther Williams Roger Williams Walter Winchell Jonathan Winters Shelley Winters Natalie Wood Peggy Wood Joanne Woodward Fay Wray Teresa Wright Jane Wyman Ed Wynn Dana Wynter **Alan Young** Gig Young Robert Young Henny Youngman Dick York

From upper left: (cw) Jeff Richards, Pat Boone, Phyliss Newman, Edd "Kookie" Burns, Anthony Franciosa

132

ACKNOWLEDGMENTS

There is a comedy routine between Lucille Ball and Carol Burnett as cleaning ladies in a theatrical office. At one point Carol Burnett says to Lucille Ball, "I'm thinking of retiring."
Lucille Ball turns around shocked and says, "And leave show business?"

After many years passed, I was hired by friends to photograph catered events, often attended by celebrities. I was amazed to find the effect hadn't diminished. I was still awed by famous people, and felt that same rush of excitement.

At an AIDs benefit at the Metropolitan Opera, Bette Midler and Liz Taylor had spoken and the Gay Men's Chorus had performed. At the after-show dinner I had photographed the table settings, flower arrangements and some of the guests; Lily Tomlin, Liz Smith, James Levine, and Yoko Ono. Informed by my friend that I was done and could leave, I didn't want to; I was back in my collecting days, still mesmerized.

The Chorus was on a balcony overlooking the dining area. They started singing, spontaneously. The acoustics were great and soon the guests joined in. We linked arms and sang patriotic songs, unashamedly and with everything we had. I was arm and arm with Ellen Burstyn and Colleen Dewhurst singing "God Bless America—I wouldn't have missed it for the world!

Acknowledgments

*One aspect of my life I haven't mentioned—it was secret.
At school I had told no one what I was up to, and until the New York Times
ran a May 2012 article about my collecting, it had remained unknown.
My fear had been that if my all male prep school classmates knew, they
would surely have made fun of me. I was already different.*

To my father for teaching me darkroom techniques when I was sixteen. And for saving my photographs
when I thought I no longer needed them. To my mother for saving my autographs when I thought I had
outgrown them. To my brother Bob, for his continued support and for always being there.

To Cooky Morales and Rosemary Yanosik for the snapshots they contributed.
My thanks as well to all the contributors we were unable to identify.

Special thanks to Skip Johnston Design for the concept and design.

My father took this portrait of me and Bob. I was 16, Bob was 7

www.ingramcontent.com/pod-product-compliance
Lightning Source LLC
Chambersburg PA
CBHW041421160426

42811CB00105B/1889